THE SPIRIT OF GREED

KENNETH BORDEAUX

THE SPIRIT OF GREED
Copyright © 2021 by Kenneth Bordeaux

All rights reserved. No part of this book may be reproduced in any form or by any electronic or mechanical means, including information storage and retrieval systems, without permission in writing from the publisher, except by reviewers, who may quote brief passages in a review.

This publication contains the opinions and ideas of its author. It is intended to provide helpful and informative material on the subjects addressed in the publication. The author and publisher specifically disclaim all responsibility for any liability, loss or risk, personal or otherwise, which is incurred as a consequence, directly or indirectly, of the use and application of any of the contents of this book.

WORKBOOK PRESS LLC
187 E Warm Springs Rd,
Suite B285, Las Vegas, NV 89119, USA

Website:	https://workbookpress.com/
Hotline:	1-888-818-4856
Email:	admin@workbookpress.com

Ordering Information:
Quantity sales. Special discounts are available on quantity purchases by corporations, associations, and others. For details, contact the publisher at the address above.

ISBN-13:	978-1-956017-58-8 (Paperback Version)
	978-1-956017-57-1 (Digital Version)

REV. DATE: 05.11.2021

Contents

Acknowledgements v
Introduction vii

Chapter One   The History of Greed 1
Chapter Two   Where does Greed come from? 9
Chapter Three   What will Greed do to you? 17
Chapter Four   How do I know if I have a spirit
                  of Greed? 23
Chapter Five   Greed in Relationships 33
Chapter Six   Greed in Raising Children 49
Chapter Seven   Greed in Marriage 65
Chapter Eight   Greed in the lyrics of Music 73
Chapter Nine   Greed in Business and Corporate
                  America 85
Chapter Ten   Watch out for Greed in your Neighbors 93
Chapter Eleven   Greed, Jealousy and Government 99

Prayer of Salvation 115

Acknowledgements

I would first like to thank my heavenly Father who is the Alpha and Omega, beginning and the end for calling me over 25 years ago to such a mighty work, a work that *"no eyes have seen no ears of have heard, no human mind have conceived, the things that God has prepared for those who love Him" (2 Corinthians 9)*. Father, you could have called so many others to do the work that you asked me to do, but you asked me instead. I felt so unqualified at the time, but I realized that you still *"choose the foolish things of the world to shame the wise; God chooses the weak things of the world to shame the strong. God chooses the lowly things and the despised things-and the things that are not to nullify the things that are, so that no one may boast before Him (1 Corinthians 1:27-29)."* I thank you for gifting me to write *"Choose, Choose II, Everybody Needs a Coach* and now, *"The Spirit of Greed"* to make an impact on the lives of your people.

Secondly, I like to thank my Lord and Savior, Jesus Christ for giving me the revelation and insight for every chapter. I had no idea how diverse and destructive that greed runs ramped in and around our lives. It was you who made me aware that it was the Spirit of Greed that was all around me and causing so much trouble in my life several years ago. I would have never thought of such thing on my own volition, I was too distracted by the trouble and pain at hand. Thank you Lord for showing me and teaching me what was really going on so that I could overcome it and later write this book to help other see through the chaos, confusion and pain that is happening in their own lives and deal with it accordingly.

Lastly, I like to thank the third part of the Godhead, the Holy Spirit. I know that you are not an "it" or a "thing," but a person. Thank you for leading and guiding me into all truth and moving on my behalf to get this book written, published and distributed. There were so many attacks, roadblocks and delays over the past 10 years to see this project pulled together, but it was your going before me that paved the way and got me over multiple hurdles and setbacks to finish. Once again, I thank you for your presence and companionship in my life, you have fought many wars together along side of me and I appreciated you, the Holy Spirit, very much in my life.

Introduction

"Have nothing to do with the fruitless deeds of darkness, but rather expose them." Ephesians 5:11

In the short time of life on earth we get a chance to observe a few things that we see is a problem and harming mankind. We all know there are wars, violence, terrorism, poverty, sexual immorality, drugs, alcohol, racism and the like in the world. All these things shake us up and cause us grief when we are confronted with it. Consequently, there is another enemy that tends to lurk in our homes, businesses, workplaces, churches, marriages, relationships, politics and legislation - it's the *Spirit of Greed.* From a young boy to my adult age I have learned to pay attention to things that go unnoticed to most and have watched what greed does to us as men and women. When a person feels like they do not have enough or should have more, you would be surprised at what comes out of them in order to make up the difference. I have seen greed operate in the vilest, meek, elite and sophisticated people. Greed has no boundaries! It does not discriminate class, culture, sex or creed. Greed will consume and destroy the life of the youngest to the oldest soul. Many fall each day as its victims. The one thing that one must understand about greed is that once you become one of its prey you are headed on a road that will lead your life to destruction. People who are bound with the spirit of greed pierce themselves with much grief, worry and manipulation in order to stay ahead. They normally have a victim mentality and justify their schemes based on their own reality of the world that has not been gracious to them.

I am very motivated to write to you on this subject. This is an enemy that needs to be exposed and needs to be pulled up at its roots. By the end of this book, you will be empowered to recognize if this spirit in your life and steer far away from it. I know that there may be a possibility that a lot of chaos is happening or has happened around your life. This book, in many cases, will help you to be able to diagnose, understand and troubleshoot what is happening around you.

The scriptures teach us in *1 Timothy 6:10, For the love of money is a root of all kinds of evil.* When evil is erupting all around you it is most likely the *love of money* or *greed* is ever present. Unfortunately, this is a spirit that those who have been or are being ensnared by it can-not easily detect. Greed is subtle and hard to discern. It can be camouflage in so many ways. For example; let's look at what Jesus once said to a young man who approached him about the dividing of the inheritance that his brother was not sharing with him. In *Luke 12:13-15*; the parable of the rich fool, reads, '*someone in the crowd said to him, "Teacher, tell my brother to divide the inheritance with me." Jesus replied, "Man, who appointed me a judge or an arbiter between you?" Then he said to them, "Watch out! Be on your guard against* **all kinds of greed***; a man's life does not consist in the abundance of his possessions."*

To the average ear, what this young man asked of Jesus did not sound like it was a bad request. Nevertheless, to Jesus, he knew exactly what this young man's real problem. It was greed lurking at his door. It will be to our benefit to spend some time studying and investigating this scripture and the aspects of greed.

Therefore, take the journey with me as I uncover and expose one of the most destructive, divisive and problematic spirits that is in the world today. The Great Apostle John warned us before his death *"For all that is in the world, the lust of the flesh, the lust of the eyes and the boasting of what he has and does" (1 John 2:16)."* Firstly, let me caution you to not interpret that I am against those who have prosperity, blessings and possessions in their life. That is not my intentions in writing on this subject. We live in a world where there are child soldiers killing adults in order to allow diamonds to be smuggled out of Africa to Europe - we have a problem. When we live in a society where kids as young as 14 years old can lay in a casket with red or blue colors on and you look around the funeral parlor and see the mother, grandmother, girlfriend, family and friends wearing the same colors - we have a problem. When we have a government that promises to increase small business owner's interest and working people investments, only to find out the rich on Wall Street get richer and the average American can-not afford to put gas in their car we have problems. The list can go on and on.

What I am writing about is a spirit that has been plaguing our society since the conception of this world. It visits in every home, business, church, relationship, marriage, community and government. I believe that God loves his people with all his heart and wants us to prosper in abundance. We must learn how to do this without the spirit of greed in any area of our lives that will make us foolish and destructive. The Apostle John wrote *"Beloved, I wish above all things that thou mayest prosper and be in health, even as thy soul prospers" (3 John 1:2).* Take notice that the first word is *" Beloved".* It means that we are well loved. The problem is that we don't understand how much the Father loves us. We think that He can't love us that much and prosper us after we look at the history of our lives. Therefore, for us to believe the promise of prosperity is rather difficult. We must know as God's people, He really does love us. He doesn't love what we do that is sinful, but He loves us very much and wants us to do well in the earth. This is the true nature of any real Father. Many of you who are parents know what I am talking about. It's hard for our children to understand that we love them even though we don't approve of what they do that is destructive. To be honest with you, a lot of children don't understand their parents who are willing to admonish what they do that is wrong. Our Father God has the same nature. He loves us. He wants us to prosper and be in good health like any Father would want for his sons and daughters. But, He will not tolerate our disobedience and foolishness. Once we get this in our thick heads, then we can understand how much God wants his blessings in our lives. You have to want God's blessing in your life more than you want to be right in your own eyes.

In today's world view, if you stand against foolishness, you can be very easily accused of being an unloving, hate-mongering and politically incorrect person. In the same way, God disciplines his children. My mother and uncle loved me and my siblings, but refused to put up with our foolishness with a belt. That was their love for all of us. Greed will make you commit many foolish acts. A person will begin to make choices and take risk that will set them up for a life time of disappointments. Again, I want to make it clear. God loves his children and he wants us to prosper in every way imaginable. My purpose in writing this book is to expose the spirit that is keeping us from doing just that, *to prosper and be in good health*. It's destroying our homes, families, marriages, relationships, businesses, hopes, dreams, goals, morals, ethics, values, culture and common sense. Let us spend some time together and explore the real enemy that wants to destroy our souls and that is – *"The Spirit of Greed."*

Chapter One
The History of Greed

"You were blameless in your ways from the day you were created till wickedness was found in you, through your widespread trade you were filled with violence, and you sinned". Ezekiel 28:15-16"So, I threw you to the earth; I made a spectacle of you before kings. By your many sins and dishonest trade you have desecrated your sanctuaries." (Ezekiel 28:18)

The Spirit of Greed has always been around, including in heaven, before the beginning of time. The prophet, Ezekiel, in his book, Chapter 28 gives us a detailed depiction of the insurrection that God had to deal with because of Lucifer's greed for more wealth, power and prestige. It is amazing that Satan would become corrupted angel in heaven after God had previously given him so much. God had given Satan great wisdom, knowledge, power, position and understanding like no other angel in heaven, only for Satan to use it to gain wealth for himself. The bible says, *"By your wisdom and understanding you have gained wealth for yourself and amassed gold and silver in your treasuries. By your great skill in trading you have increased your wealth, and because of your wealth, your heart has grown proud"* Ezekiel 28:4-5. Although he had it all, Satan proved to God and the rest of the heavenly host that he could not handle prosperity. The drive to gain more consumed him and wickedness was found in his heart. My question is what was that wickedness or iniquity found in his heart? I appeal to you that it was Greed! Satan had plenty, but it wasn't enough. Let's look again at what the bible say's Satan had:

"You were the model of perfection, full of wisdom and perfect in beauty. You were in Eden, the garden of God; every precious stone adorned you: ruby, topaz and emerald, chrysolite, onyx and jasper, sapphire, turquoise and beryl. Your settings and mountings were made of gold; on the day you were created they were prepared. You were anointed as a guardian cherub, so I ordained you. You were on the holy mount of God; you walked among the fiery stones. You were blameless in your ways from the day you were created. You were blameless in your ways from the day you were created till wickedness was found in you, through your widespread trade you were filled with violence, and you sinned" Ezekiel 28:1216. From this passage, we can see the spirit of greed has been in existence before the creation of the world. It was found in heaven. Satan had it all and wanted more. He had every precious stone embedded within him and still he was not a satisfied angel. He was the model of perfection in wisdom, understanding and beauty. He was the head of all the angels and still that was not enough. Unfortunately, when he was kicked out of heaven and thrown down to the earth by God, he transferred that spirit with him along with a third of the angels that believed in him. He focused on Adam and Eve as his next prey. He wanted them to become interested in becoming just like God. The problem with this attempt is that they were already made in the image and likeness of God. Just like Satan, God had positioned Adam and Eve in a place of authority with Him. The two of them had

it all. Adam and Eve would be the first in the earth to fall to this foul spirit. God had given Adam and Eve authority over everything in the garden except the right to eat from *the tree of knowledge of good and evil.* They could eat from any tree accept that particular one. If they did, they were warned that *"you will surely die" Genesis 2:17.*

Satan, also known as, the Serpent, convinced Eve that *"You will not surely die, for God knows that when you eat of it your eyes will be opened, and you will be like God, knowing good and evil" Genesis 3:4-5.* Satan was able to spew the same spirit that got him and one-third of the angels, kicked out of heaven into Adam and Eve. As we know the history, the two took of the tree of knowledge of good and evil and ate the forbidden fruit. At that moment, sin fell in the garden and it came on the entire posterity of man. The sin that came on the entire posterity of man was the same sin that was in Satan. Now it had entered Adam and Eve. What was that sin? Greed! This spirit has a history going back into the ancient of days. It is a spirit of dissatisfaction or not enough. It always wants, it always needs and disregards what it already has. What is it with man that we can be given so much, but yet feel like we have so little? What is it with man that we can have great position, but want more authority? What is this need to have everything and everyone under our control? How do you know when you or you are dealing with someone who has been infected with Satan's greed? You can always tell when you or that person is never satisfied. There are many people in the world that you can never satisfy. Nothing is enough! They are always murmuring, complaining, wanting, hurting, never accepting, thankful or appreciating what they have. The word *"Thank You"* eludes them. It is like pouring into a bottomless pit or feeding a brand new baby his/her bottle, always crying for more. No matter how hard you work or how hard you try, you can-not satisfy them.

Men and women like that do not take the time to enjoy what they already have before they want something else. When you are like this, you must recognize that this is a spirit that was found in Satan thousands of years ago and now is in you. It has been sent down to the earth to contaminate us all. The word of God says it this way, *"The great dragon was hurled down, that ancient serpent called the devil, or Satan, who leads the whole world astray. He was hurled to the earth, and his angels with him." Revelations 12:9.* We must understand that those angels that were sent down to the earth with Satan are no more than evil spirits; greedy, lustful - dissatisfied demons. These demons can never have enough bloodshed, violence, murder, money, sex, hatred, jealousy, power, fame, influence or control. How do you think the devil is able to lead the whole world astray? He is able to do it through a spirit that we all can be attacked with. The greed in him had the ability to come down to infect us all. Understand that the devil has one third of the angels working with him to make sure that the entire world is full of his influence. Look at our world today and its history. Have you paid any attention to the wars that have been fought for more territory? You can have this land, but you want that land too. How about the wars that are being fought over the power to control the oil? What about our nation's reluctance in taking an aggressive stand to stop illegal immigration into America? Why do we not deal with this? It is because large corporations that have political influence in Washington, DC want more cheap labor to come across our borders. Why should I pay you as American citizens $12.00 per hour, when I can pay an illegal citizen who will gladly work for $8.00 dollars per hour? Satan's weapon of greed is at an all-time high in the world today. In the book of Revelations the world has been warned. *But woe to the earth and the sea, because the devil has gone down to you! He is filled with fury, because he knows that his time is short. Revelations 12:12.* This verse alone lets us know that Satan has every motivation to corrupt the whole world due to his lack of time. The same thing that was in him he wants to put into the hearts and souls of men, women, and children. The only way he can have us is to get us to do what one third of the angels did in heaven and what Adam and Eve did in the garden and that is to listen to him. What did Jesus tell the Jews who were trying to kill him? Jesus said to them, *"If God were your Father, you would love me, for I came from God and now am here. I have not come on my own; but he sent me. Why is my language not clear to you? Because you are unable to hear what I say. You belong to your father, the devil, and you want to carry out your father's desire. He was a murderer from the beginning, not holding to the truth, for there is no truth in him. When he lies, he speaks his native language, for he is a liar and the father of lies. Yet because I tell the truth, you do not believe me!" John 8:42-45.* Satan wants us all to listen to him so we can carry out his lies', this is how he gets his will in the earth. Unfortunately, many people are doing things and living in a way that they think they are executing their own will, but have no idea that they have listened to Satan and are carrying out his will. They have been listening to him without knowing it, and they justify their actions as their own choice. A good sign of men and women who have been impacted in this way is they refuse godly council. It will go in their left ear and out the right ear. What you say will have no impact on them at all. Not to throw the mentally ill under the bus, but how many times have they reported to someone that they are hearing voices only later to carry out acts of violence that a clearly of Satan will? I was in the parking lot of the Century 16 Movie Theatre on July 20, 2012 about 3 hours before the shooting started that killed 12 people and injured 70 others. The young man that did this had reported to his psychologist that he was hearing voices and feared he would hurt someone. Who voice do you think he was hearing? I know it's not politically correct to say it in our *"user friendly"* world today, but he was hearing the voice of Satan, who is still getting man to listen to him and carry out his will.

Speaking of listening to another, look what our young people desire today. Everything that is expensive. I-pods, Ipads, I-phones, Beat headphones, Play Stations, Game Boy, XBOX, Designer Clothes, Designer Shoes, Jewelry, Guns, Cars…etc. They want all this stuff, but very few parents will make them work a part-time job to pay for any of it. Many young people today want everything accept what will advance them in character, education, discipline, morals, careers, values and respectable goals. Why does this happen? Our kids are bombarded with advertisement each day that they have no real significance in the world unless they have these desirable possessions. This is the voice that they are listening to. To make it worse, we have parents that try to give them all these things despite how terrible their grades and attendance are in school or the negative attitudes that they carry around like luggage. This makes no sense, why are we so afraid to rebuke our own children when they need it? Why are adults so busy trying to be their child's friend instead of being their parents? This is a sick as the greed in the world itself. Many in the world are falling prey to this spirit. The fallout of greed is filling up our prisons, mortuaries, graveyards, courts houses, and shelters while at the same time emptying our classrooms, churches, homes and bank accounts. If there was ever a day we needed to declare a war on greed, it is now! Who are you listening to? Realize that there is not a class of people in society that has not been tainted by greed. Greed is impartial, from the white house, to the whore house, to the crack house, to the church house, to your house and my house; we can be attacked by greed. It's going to take an army of God's people, a new nation, filled with God's Spirit to combat the greed that is having such influence in the earth. Remember, this is Satan's greatest folly and how he is deceiving the whole world today. You may not be able to fix the world, but you can fix yourself and warn your children. We must humble ourselves and get God's vision for prosperity. The Lord really does love us! He wants us to have things, but He doesn't want things to have us. If we are hungry for anything it should be for more of his spirit to shine through our lives. It is the spirit of God in our lives that is going to separate the wheat from the tears in this world. Let's not be ignorant of Satan's devices, know the history of greed and from whence it came, despising all aspects of its manifestation in our life and world today whether it's in government, business, relationships, marriage, church, politics, finances…etc.

Chapter Two

Where does Greed come from?

People who want to get rich fall into temptation and a trap and into many foolish and harmful desires that plunge men into ruin and destruction. 1Timothy 6:9

What causes fights and quarrels among you? Don't they come from your desires that battle within you? You want something but you don't get it. You kill and you covet, but you cannot have what you want. James 4:1-2

Still others, like seed sown among thorns, hear the word, but the worries of this life, the deceitfulness of wealth and the desire for other things come in and choke the word making it unfruitful. Mark 4:18-19

If you read these three scriptures carefully you will notice that each of them contains a certain word - *"desire"*. The word desire means *longing or wish*. Greed comes from a man's desire (longing or wish) that is within his heart. Another word for desire could be *"cravings."* We all know what it is like to crave certain foods. The feeling that you get at the time will not subside until you find what you want and eat it. Desire is much like craving. It will not go away until you satisfy its lust. The devil knows that if he can influence your desires that he will control your life. I find it interesting that mankind desires is high for so much stuff, but very low for God and His Kingdom. This is not by accident it is by the strategic plan and design of Satan. He wants the world to market to you what he wants you to crave. He is taking control of our longings, wishes and desires within. For example, the person who wants to get rich has his/her desires on money and possessions. This person is not concerned about morals, character, integrity, right or wrong. To them, it is all about the money. In their heart and mind, the money justifies who they are and what they do. The desire to become rich causes them to make many foolish and harmful decisions that they later regret. We must know that God's plan for wealth in your life is not for destruction, but for the good.

There are two kinds of desires that the Apostle Paul addresses the Corinthian church, *sinful* and *Spiritual*. *"Those who live according to the sinful nature have their minds set on what that nature desires; but those who live in accordance with the Spirit have their minds set on what the Spirit desires" Romans 8:5*. This is a very powerful statement that requires our attention. Let's really look at this verse. When we live towards our *sinful desires* we have our minds set on the things that that nature desires. When we live according to what the *Spirit desires,* we have our minds on the things of the Spirit. Unfortunately, what the *Spirit desires* is not something we normally want, but it is what God wants. God and His Spirit are one. What God wants is what makes the difference in our lives. If we don't spend time finding out what the Spirit desires, then all our energy is toward what the flesh desires – which is greed! This is how greed sneaks into our hearts. We don't desire what the Spirit wants. How many of us have been taught that the Spirit has a desire? We are not taught to be led by our spirit, but by our flesh. The word teaches *"For those who are led by the spirit (of God) are the children of God"* (Romans 8:14). Being led by the Spirit of God is not an easy thing to consistently live by. What may look like to others that you have no idea of where you are heading, they have no idea that you are right in the epicenter of the plan of God for your life.

Our desires must come from the Spirit of God. If not, we will crave things that are not the will of God for our lives. I have done it. We all have done it. God gives man a free will. He doesn't dictate to us what we should desire or not desire, but He gives us an opportunity to desire what the Spirit desires. We can have victory over greed if we approach life this way. Again, I will not tell you that it is an easy road to desire what the Spirit desires at all times. Many times desiring what is right will come at a price. I can tell you that you will experience setbacks, backlashes, criticisms and attacks that stem from greed, bitterness, hatred, jealousy and anger from other people. They will deal with you in this way because you all of a sudden, do not want what they want, but what God wants. As long as you want what they want, you are in a good place with them. But, as soon as your appetite changes for what the Spirit wants, they will not want what you want and therefore, not want you anymore. This was the problem that Jesus had with the Jews that wanted to kill him? They had a devilish desire to kill him. All the while they thought they were Abraham's children. Jesus wanted something that they did not have a desire for and that was the will of his Father. The Jews saw what Jesus was saying about the resurrection and the miracles he was doing as foolishness. What you will see as God's will, the world will see as foolishness. The scriptures read, *"The man without the*

Spirit does not accept the things that come from the Spirit of God, for they are foolishness to him, and he cannot understand them, because they are spiritually discerned" 1 Corinthians 2:14. This is how you can have two Christians in a relationship and they are unequally yoked. One has the Spirit the other is carnal (led by his/her own will, reasoning and emotions). It will not work!

Therefore, we must understand what the Spirit desires and can do for us. It will ultimately keep us from the desires of this world. The world and its desires will not last forever. The Apostle John wrote, *"The world and its desires will pass away, but the man who does the will of God lives forever" 1 John 2:17.* Another way to read this verse is: *"The world and its desires pass away, but the man who desires what the Spirit desires will live forever."* I personally believe that long life comes with being led by the Spirit. God wants us to be able to do His will, the good works that he has prepared for us in advance *(see Ephesians 2:10).* In order to do the will of God you have to desire it in your life. This is not something that just happens, your spirit has to seek it and desire it. God's will is in his Word. We must not desire anything less than His Word in our life. No one has to accept the devil's desire by listening to him for his/her life. Satan has a desire too! Once we see him planting his mouth in our life, we can resist it. The scripture teach, *"Resist the devil and he will flee from you" James 4:7.* Therefore, it is important that what is in our hearts is from the Spirit of God, if it is, then we have been promised that we will receive the desires of our hearts. The book of Psalms say's, *Delight yourself in the Lord, and he will give you the desires of your heart" Psalm 37:4.* We can receive evil desires in our hearts just as well as God's desires. We have to choose which desire we want. For example, desiring to be married can be earthly; desiring to have a godly marriage that impacts the world around you (and nothing less) is spiritual and is what God desires for his son's and daughter's.

The Prophet Isaiah gives us some clues into what the Israelites desired in their hearts thousands of years ago to keep from being corrupted by this world. The Israelites in Isaiah's day desired four key things: walking in the way of the law of the Lord, waiting for Him, His Name, and His renown. Here is what they said, *"Yes, Lord, walking in the way of your laws, we wait for you; your name and renown are the desire of our hearts" Isaiah 26:8.* God's renown is his fame and high distinction. We are to desire his Word, waiting for Him, His name, and His high distinction. It would be good to see people get back to having high honor and distinction for God. There is so much disrespect and dishonor for God in the world today. How many of us have ever been taught that this is what we should desire in our hearts? Can you imagine the difference in our nation if this is what we are taught through television, radio, parents, schools, magazines, and billboards? If this is what we are supposed to desire? It would change the entire climate of our world. Instead of producing greed and division we would be producing righteous seed. The devil doesn't want righteous seed in the earth. He hates it. He can't stand righteous people in the world. The righteous are no more than targets to be taken out. He wants a corrupt seed (people) in the earth. He wants to master and control them with material things that have no eternal value. Again, I am not coming against prosperity and those who have it. What I am coming against is the greed that controls the mind, will, and emotions of man. Satan always uses evil desires in order to trap you. Solomon said, *"The righteousness of the upright delivers them, but the unfaithful are trapped by evil desires" Proverbs 11:6.* Make no mistakes; the unfaithful are always entangled by their evil desires. Their desires stem from the spirit of greed. It is sad to see when people get caught in its web. Even though you can see it, the person cannot see what has gotten a hold of them. They may think that this is the way they are, but do not realize that this is not the way God has intended for them to live. Consequently, many will justify not changing or repenting from their evil desires. It is easier for them to accept themselves as the way they are because greed is so strong inside of them. You must understand that your wants have very little or nothing to do with the will of God and what He has planned for your life. The wants or desires that are in you could have come from an influence of the world. We all should lay our desires down to be crucified before God. The scriptures teach that, *"Those who belong to Christ Jesus have crucified the sinful nature with its passions and desires. Since we live by the Spirit, let us keep in step with the Spirit" Galatians 5:24-25.* When our desires have been crucified, then we too have been crucified. When we get to the place in our minds that it's not what we want, but what He wants, we can trust that we are heading in the right direction. Take for example the writing of this kingdom minded book. It was never my desire to write Christian books. If you don't believe me, find some of my old friends where I grew up in Rochester, New York and they will tell you. "No, I don't think those were his plans." Your old friends know you before you changed and start living for God. They knew you when you were filled with the passion and lust of the world. This is not what I wanted to do. I'm not saying that we all need to write Christian books, do gospel music, preach or teach. What I am saying is whatever you do, it should be inspired by God. You may ask; if writing Christian books was not your desire, what happened? God changed my desires to His desires. The

Apostle Paul said it like this, *"I have been crucified with Christ and I no longer live, but Christ lives in me. The life I live in the body, I live by faith in the Son of God who loved me and gave himself for me" Galatians 2:20.* It's not my life anymore, it's His.

In conclusion, if we are going to combat the Spirit of Greed and where it comes from, then we are going to have to wage war on our desires that are of ourselves and not of God. This is why church attendance is so important. The house of God is where we hear the Word of God and the Will of God preached. Believe me; the world without the church will be in total chaos. Regardless of what you have experienced in your life, find the church that God has for you. **"Get where you are supposed to be!"** Is what my Pastor, Dr. Mark T. Bagwell said to me the first time I visited his church the early 90s. He was right. God has a place for all of us to learn and grow in the Spirit. It is at this place where you will find the Word that brings your desires into His desires. Don't leave it up to your flesh to do so. *"Get where you are supposed to be"* and be transformed into the glory of his dear Son.

Chapter Three

What will Greed do to you?

Some people, eager for money, have wandered from the faith and pierced themselves with many griefs. 1Timothy 6:10

The reason why Christians should be concerned about the Spirit of Greed is that many have wandered away from the faith behind it. Anything that can lead God's people away from the faith should be a major concern of ours. Remember, it is Satan's desire to get you wanting something other than the will of God for your life. His whole purpose is to cause you to wander away from God's word. When people wander, they walk around not knowing who they are, what they have, what they are looking for or where they are going. They are lost! The Israelites wandered in the wilderness for 40 years. They had no idea of what they had in Jehovah-Jared. The people murmured and complained in the desert desiring to return back to Egypt as slaves. They reasoned in their hearts that it would be better to return back to slavery. They wanted to be able to enjoy the leeks, onions and melons they were privileged to eat in Egypt no longer wanting the manna in the desert that God provided. Here's my point, the Spirit of Greed is causing many to wander around in a wilderness desiring the wrong things. They do not know who they are, who's they are, where they are going and who they are serving. To wander means to go aimlessly from place to place, meander, or stray from the path. When we are in the faith, it means that our eyes are fixed on where we are going and who is leading us. The writer in the book of Hebrews said, *"Let us fix your eyes on Jesus, the author and finisher of our faith" (Hebrews 12:2)*. We should have our aim and direction fixed on the Kingdom of God and Christ. The Spirit of Greed causes us to lose that focus and therefore end up wandering from where we should be.

Greed causes us to lose all sense of reason and consciousness of our surroundings. To be conscious means to be awake, alert and aware of what's going on. The key words here are *awake, alert* and *aware*. The love of money has a way of making you lose your good sense and awareness. You will find yourself involved in things that you would have never done in your right mind. I have talked to people who have done some things they regret behind the love of money - greed. Each of them had a similar testimony that they were not thinking in their right mind at the time. They testify that they were so consumed with getting money that it dominated their thoughts. Crimes of all types will happen. Let's understand a lot of men and women who are in prison are not all evil people. Many of them got between a rock and a hard place and were not thinking right when they broke the law to gain money. The bible calls it *"ill-gotten gain" (Proverbs 10:2)*. So you know; I am not trying to make excuses for anyone who has broken the law for money? What I am trying to prove is that you can lose your mind going after ill-gotten gain. We all can be tempted! There is not much difference between those of us who have not a record from those who do, some just never got caught. Greed can tempt the noblest of mind in our society. Why? Because it is a spirit and a spirit is free to roam anywhere it can take up residents. This is why we hear news reports of very bright people doing some extremely dumb acts. I say again, that they were not using their brain at the time and moved forward with wicked schemes that they felt they could get away with. I know of men who have lost their wives behind acts of greed for financial gain. It's not that they were not good people, they got themselves mixed up with the wrong crowd and went after the money. The important fact to know is that greed will make you lose your right mind. The things you will do today, you would wonder how you ever got involved in such foolishness tomorrow.

Many are conducting under handed schemes in order to gain wealth. Whether it is white or blue collar crimes, it's all about getting rich quick. Greed has no boundaries. We can get a clear picture about the very nature of greed by reading the story about Naaman. He needed to be healed of leprosy by the prophet Elisha. After receiving his healing, Naaman insisted that the prophet Elisha receive gifts of silver, gold, and clothing for healing him. The prophet Elisha refused to receive the gifts for it was not the time to do such a thing. Despite Elisha's refusal to receive any gifts, his servant, Gehazi, hurried after Naaman and made up a lie so that he would send back some of the gifts with him to give to Elisha. In truth, the Spirit of Greed was upon Gehazi and he wanted the gifts for himself. Because of Gehazi's greed, the prophet Elisha's found out about it and pronounced Naaman's leprosy now cling to him and his descendants forever. Gehazi was from that point, leprous as white as snow. Greed will make you lose your consciousness of God's purpose. Gehazi was not awake, alert or aware of his surroundings that the spirit of Elisha was with him when Naaman got down from his chariot to meet with him. The prophet Elisha addressed Gehazi;

"Where have you been, Gehazi?" Your servant didn't go anywhere, Gehazi answered. But Elisha said to him, "Was not my spirit with you when the man got down from his chariot to meet you? Is this the time to take money, or to accept clothes, olive groves, vineyards, flocks, herds, or menservants and maidservants? 2 Kings 5:25-26. A lot of our experiences of greed are like this example. We do things that we should not, not realizing that those who we are spiritually connected to God know when we have done something that we should not. As parents, we call it intuition. I don't care how much your kids try to keep certain things away from your knowledge you know when they have done something or are doing something that they should not be doing. It is revealed to you in your spirit as if you were right there. It is the same way with God. He knows everything that we do and when we do it. It is a deceptive spirit of greed that makes us think that we can get away with what we ought not. Greed is a choice that many people make on their own volition, but not in their right mind. No matter how much you try to reach, persuade, and encourage others to stay away from the power of greed, you find many falling head long into one of Satan's most deceptive traps. It's one thing when youth get caught up in the spirit of Greed, it's another thing when adults get entangled and display the spirit to the young. The word of God is clear that we are to *"Flee the evil desires of youth," 2 Timothy 2:22.* It is when we are children that we want what we want and do anything to get it. Unfortunately, there are adults that still have that spirit in them. If they can't get what they want, they whine, cry, lie, rob, steal, and kill in order to get it. Timothy was told, *"But you, man of God, flee from all this" 1 Timothy 6:11.* The proper exit from greed is to flee from it. You can't just walk away from greed and all that it brings. This is the reason why it is so hard for those

who have tasted the sweetness of ill-gotten gain. They have seen the money come in quickly and in large amounts. These people know what it's like to make as much in a day then most people will see in months. It is very difficult for them to refrain from falling back into this sin. It is a trap. To be clear, they are addicted to this form of living and are in need of deliverance. Deceived, they have opened themselves up to a spirit that will now not give them a day's rest. They have the *"I got to have it now."* Regardless of the risk or cost, they must have what they want. Unfortunately, nothing will stop them getting what they want. One reading this would say, this sounds a lot like me, how do I get free from it? Hold on, I will not leave you hanging. I will discuss that later. The point that we need to know at this time is that the spirit of Greed will make you lose consciousness. Your life will be out of control. It will be governed by a spirit that has no intentions of letting you go.

This is why I believe that people become repeat offenders. Even though they have spent time in prison, the spirit that put the person in the prison in the first place has no intentions of letting them go. No sooner than the person is released back into society they are right back in prison. This is a serious thing that one must take into careful consideration if they are going to thrive and be alive. The longer the devil can control you, the more grief, pain, and destruction he can cause you and others who are in your life. I'm telling you, the devil has got a hold of a lot of men, women, and children with a strong appetite to do whatever it takes to *"get theirs."* Have you ever heard a person say *"I'm going to get mines?"* If you have, that's a dangerous spirit talking. Others are more covert in what they do in order to get what they want. They don't openly say "I'm going to get mines", but what they do in their hearts is even more destructive. They don't look the part, but they are just as dangerous. The ones who are bound the most by this spirit are the self- righteous who cover it up, but are very deceitful. Maybe they have not had such a background or life that involved gangs, drugs, violence… etc. But what they don't know is that this spirit doesn't start and stop in the ghetto, it starts in the mind. This spirit is in the suburbs, country clubs, mountains, valleys, church, pews, pulpit, corporate office, public office, doctor's office, law office, dental office, pastor's office…etc.

Lastly, let's look at what Jeremiah the prophet said *"From the least to the greatest, all are greedy for gain prophets and priests alike, all practice deceit" Jeremiah 6:13*. The point is that Satan does not only have the ghettos of this world bound with greed, he has the upper echelons and the elites of society, including many in the church. I say, watch your cravings and desires of this world. Watch what you run after! Do not let the devil destroy the joy and bliss that we all can receive in God's prosperity by being bound with a spirit of Greed. I expect to be blessed. I believe in being blessed. I know God wants to bless. God has blessed me. I don't want to spend a lot of time with anyone who doesn't believe in being blessed by God. It is God who blesses his children. He knows how to bless you without you selling your soul to the devil in order to be blessed. In our blessings, we should be conscious of our God. He will bless you so that you can be a blessing to others and he will receive the glory for your blessing. He made the promise to Abram, *"I will make you into a great nation and I will bless you; I will make your name great and you will be a blessing" Genesis 12:2*. The last I looked in the bible, the church is still the seed of Abraham. The promise that he made to Abraham is now ours through adoption by Jesus Christ. Go and get your blessings from Lord, but don't ever get tainted with the "Spirit of Greed." There is no need!

Chapter Four

How do I know if I have a spirit of Greed?

What causes fights and quarrels among you? Don't they come from your desires that battles within you? You want something but don't get it. You kill and covet, but you cannot have what you want. You quarrel and fight. James 4:1-2(NIV) From whence comes wars and fightings among you? Come they not hence, even of your lusts that war in your members? Ye lust and have not: ye kill, and desire to have, and cannot obtain: ye fight and war. James 4:1-2 (KJV)

I stated James 4:1-2 above in both the New International Version and King James translations because what I am going to discuss in this chapter is very important. One thing I have learned about Christians is that when the Pastor begins to discuss a topic that is not favorable, they immediately reject it and say to them-selves *"that's not for me."* But I challenge you to hear me out in this chapter because it may save you from certain destructive behavior. If there was a verse of scripture that the Apostle James talked about that describes the essence of what is going on inside of men and women when we don't understand that person's attitude or behavior, it is written in James 4:1-2. Before I came into the knowledge of Jesus Christ at age 20, I always thought that Christians were different from the rest of the people in the world. Wow, was I open for a rude awakening! I thought that a Christian man or woman was a peaceful person who didn't like chaos, confusion, arguments, combativeness, fighting or conflict. I discouragingly found out that what I was thinking was not true. I realized that Christians or people who go to Church (however you want to put it) are just as difficult, argumentative and combative as any other group of people on the face of the earth. In fact, one of the reasons I became a Christian and started going to church is because I wanted to have a peace of mind and minimum conflict as possible in my life. I thought, maybe being around calm, non-combative, peaceful and loving people was what I was missing in my life. The truth of the matter is that saints love to quarrel and fight just as much as anyone else in the world. Quarreling and fighting has nothing to do with whether a person is attending church. The portrait painted of Believer's is normally that they are peaceful, respectful, loving, and kind people. What Christians don't know is that much of the world is drawn to them because when they get tired of how they are living, they see the peace and solace that they think Christians have and want to be a-part of it. To much of their surprise, this is a lot of times a front. It has nothing to do with who these people are on the inside. In my early 20s, I lived around Christian groups like the Quakers, Mennonites, and the Amish. I had a year tour in Korea and lived with South Koreans who had converted from Buddhism to Christianity. Both of these opportunities were good for me as a new Christian. I would testify that I noticed that all three groups were clearly very peaceful, loving, respectful and kind people. They were different and had their problems like anyone else, but over-all peace-loving people. That being said, I understand that these groups are not the norm that most of us will experience. I only experienced these groups because of my time served in the U.S. Air Force. I believe that God wanted me to learn something about my faith early on that would make a difference in my life later. Most of our American experience is living among the Baptist, Methodist, Presbyterian, Pentecostal, Charismatic, Catholic, Episcopalian, Lutheran, Non-Denominational, Evangelical, African American AME, Church of Christ, Church of God In Christ...etc. My first six months as a Christian was in a Baptist Church. I was very happy to be with God's people, but I would notice something shortly that was not much different from the world I had just left. The people in the church choir were very argumentative, disrespectful and uncooperative with the choir director. I did not know that church folk act in that way. I didn't understand spiritual and carnal at that time, but was kind of shocked at what I was witnessing as a new believer. It seemed like every week, somebody had an attitude towards the director, a soloist, or another member. In fact, some of the people in the congregation treated each other very unfriendly and would not speak to one another. I watched this for only a few months in Colorado then was shipped off to South Korea and started experiencing the Korean Christians culture along with American Believers that were stationed overseas. If I thought the Christians in America were interesting, it was nothing to be compared to what I would see and learn about American Christians oversees. It was like a night and day the difference when it came to the focus of life between American Christians and the Korean Christians. I want you to really hear me on this, these things had a real impact on me as a 20 year old learning about Christ. A lot of things I saw not only blew my mind, but taught me what really mattered as a believer early on. Remember, I was a new born, still a babe in

Christ, only 6 months saved. I would use this time that I was going to be in Korea (a full year) to study and learn from both groups, the Americans and the Koreans. I noticed that bowing and being respectful was a-part of Korean customs and courtesy. Therefore, when I would meet a Korean Christian at church, they would bow to express their sincere love and respect for me as a brother in Christ. I would bow back to them with the same respect and appreciation. This was so different to me. I was an urban inner-city kid *"Straight Out of Rochester,"* people did not bow to nobody there for any reason. Doing something like that would probably get you beat up and robbed real fast. I noticed that the Korean believers treated all of the American Christians with respect, almost like royalty. It was a weird feeling for me, but it was real. I can't explain it, all I can say is that it was the first time I felt angelic or something like it. Again, it was weird. I wanted to tell them, *"No, No, Its ok, I'm human just like you."* What I did not realize is that it was their custom to be a servant to others. That would be the dividing line between the two groups that I would realize and understand. In one country people are taught to be servants. In another country people are taught to be about themselves. My experience with the American Christians overseas was quiet different with the Korean Christians. I will never forget what I learned there and it became the foundation of my Christian faith, *"never let anyone pump you up to being bigger than a servant to others."* That being said, I have to talk to you about an incident that happened while I was over there that makes my point. After a month into my year tour, the Lord blessed me with a good Christian friend from South Carolina, country boy named *"Stan."* Stan and I would become good friends. Can you imagine that, country boy and inner-city kid? Tell me God don't have a sense of humor. Stan and I were both baby Christians and newly married to young ladies back in the states.

He had been in Korea a month longer than I, had been saved a month longer than I, and had been married a month longer than I. What a coincidence? Stan worked in the motor pool, therefore had access to the military vehicles during off duty hours with the permission of his supervisor. The church that we attended was on the other side of the city of Taegu City (a city of over 3 million people). Stan would transport the American Christians from our base to church service held at Camp Walker Army base on the other side of Taegu City. I normally rode up front with Stan since he would come and get me first. Our church service was called the *"Gospel Hour"* since it was mixed with Baptist, Church of God in Christ, Catholics, Lutherans, Pentecostals and South Koreans. We had no real Pastor due to our location and so much turn-over within each year. Whoever knew the most about the bible pretty much became the Pastor during their stay. That ruled my-self and Stan out since we were new to Christ. Trust me; the American Christians let us both know when they had the chance that we were babes. To me, it was a joke. Little did Stan and I know at the time this would be the best place for the both of us. We would find out why the bible teaches, *"Believers in humble circumstances should take pride in their high position" (James 1:9)*. The carnality that would go on amongst the American Christians was crazy and embarrassing. Many times either in the pulpit, in the van on the way to church or after church, in the restaurants, there would be some very heated argument about doctrine, clothing, make-up, music, speaking in tongues and the like amongst the American Christians. Stan and I normally sat quietly and smiled at each other because we weren't going to get into it at all. We knew they would just shut us down because we didn't know as much about the bible as the rest of them. We thought that they all were crazy. I would feel real bad when the American Christians would do this in front of the

Korean Christians and guest we would invite to church. Again, I didn't have lots' of bible knowledge at the time, but I had good sense. I knew right from wrong. To me and Stan it was out of place. It got so bad at times that I remember we would want to separate our-selves from the American Christians. There was a particular Korean Christian man always in our services. His name was Mr. Hahn. He was a very humble man whom gained our attention as new believers. One day during a Martin Luther King celebration week. Mr. Hahn asked us to sing at a Korean Christian church that he was connected to. Due to the turnover because of a short one year tour for each of us, I eventually ended up being the choir director for a moment. Up until this time, we only had Koreans visit and attend the Gospel Hour. Mr. Hahn had taken all of us out to a fine restaurant that evening before we went to the Korean Church to sing. We had a good time and the food was great. He had paid for everyone's meal himself and had a few Korean friends with him. We sat on the floor and ate the way Korean's do. We left the restaurant and followed Mr. Hahn to the Korean Church. I was up front, like usual, with Stan. Stan and I couldn't believe what we started to hear in the passenger section of the van. The American Christians, once again started arguing about speaking in tongues, should a women wear pants, long skirts or make-up in church. Here we just were treated to a good meal by Mr. Hahn and on our way to sing at a Korean Church he invited us to. I loved Mr. Hahn and was honored to go and do this for him. It was a hot mess. After a while I had had enough and I started to say something to all of them in the back. I was so mad. Stan knew me and saw that I was getting ready to give them all a piece of my mind. He said, *"Ken, stay out of it. Don't get into it."* They kept on and after a-while they all were mad and upset at each other. After a few minutes, we all noticed than van slowing down as we were nearing a Korean community we had never been. Mr. Hahn, in his car a head of us started leading us down these very narrow and congested side streets. We had not been on streets like this before. It was like we had just entered into a different world it was clear that everyone started being concerned as to where we were going. It was a different part of the city that didn't look like the rest. We were definitely in even a more impoverished area of the country. Mr. Hahn turned down a few more very narrow side streets as we got deeper into the community with a lot of people and kids walking very close to our van. The people were looking inside of it at us. They were smiling as if they were expecting us. You could tell that these Koreans had not really seen a lot of Americans before. When we parked and got out of the van, Mr. Hahn walked back to us and led us to where we were going. We were kind of afraid and confused; we didn't see a Church building only an impoverished torn down neighborhood with lots of people. It was one way into this community and one way out. There was nothing but slums to our left and right. Mr. Hahn led us into this apartment building with a really tight door way and down some stairs that looked like a basement. At the bottom of these stairs was a door that when it was opened, there was a large Church sanctuary with more Koreans smiling, bowing, taking our coats, offering us *"Coke"* and welcoming us. We were all shocked! They hugged us, bowed to us, and honored us so highly that we couldn't stand it. Stan and I looked at each other and smirked because we knew all the foolishness our American Christian brothers and sisters were just involved in and knew they were mad at each other and now this was happening to them. It was crazy. It took everything within Stand and I to keep from busting out laughing. These Korean Christians loved on us so well that they knew they did not deserve it. Stan and I never saw them so humbled. We sat in the service with Korean Christians and the only words we could understand was Amen and Hallelujah. After their Pastor preached we would be called up to sing several selections. I will never forget the smirk on my friends Stan's face in baritone section. He and I knew that God had stepped in that situation, caught them off guard, and shut all of them up. I was so glad. I couldn't stand it anymore. They all wanted to be right and God showed them that they all were wrong. That night we saw that Christianity was not about speaking in tongues, what to wear, not to wear, lipstick or make-up. It was about serving Him and one another. I never forgot it. It became the foundation of my Christian walk. God taught me this himself. It's about serving others. It's religion that makes us attack each other, that's why I refuse to be religious. I saw what it does to people. It makes them mean, hateful and self-righteous. If God had no other purpose for bringing me to Korea but to make this point clear to me early in my Christian walk, then it was more than worth the trip. After singing a few more songs and again being very well treated by the Korean Christians. We left the Church and boarded the van. Mr. Hahn led us out of the tight community. We didn't know at the time, but we had been in one of the original underground churches in South Korea before Christianity was openly accepted. This is where Christians would worship in secret for fear of imprisonment or death. Buddhism was the pre-dominate religion before the Korean War for many years. Therefore, these people appreciated the gospel that was brought over to them by the Americans during and after the war. They had great respect and high regard for anyone connected to Christ. You should have seen Korean Christian faces. They were so thankful that South Korea had accepted Christianity and they did not have to hide anymore in worship. The other great thing I would never forget about that night is the long ride back. It was so quiet on that van that you could hear a pin drop. Stan and I kept looking at each other all the way home talking with our eyes. We could not believe what we had just witnessed as baby Christians, not even a year saved. Tell me that God will not shut the mouth of the prideful. It made an impact on us both. We saw that God was all powerful and He knew how to handle a situation when He needed to. We learned that Christianity is truly meant to be a peace-loving, kind and service orientated faith. The Korean's had it and the American's didn't. The Korean Christians treated us better than we treated each other. The Apostle James says' it this way,

"Who is wise and understanding among you? Let him show it by his good life, by deeds done in the humility that comes from wisdom. But if you harbor bitter envy and selfish ambition in your hearts, do not boast about it or deny the truth. Such "wisdom" does not come down from heaven but is earthly, unspiritual, of the devil. For where you have envy and selfish ambition, there you find disorder and every evil practice. But the wisdom that comes from heaven is first of all pure then peace-loving, considerate, submissive, full of mercy and good fruit, impartial and sincere. Peacemakers who sow in peace raise a harvest of righteousness" James 3:13-17.

It was clear to me that night there was *"bitter envy and selfish ambition"* in our circle of saints and God stepped into kill it. The temptation to influence the group with each other's doctrinal and traditional beliefs was ridiculous and extreme. Disorder and confusion stemmed from greed and a desire for power to influence the whole group. Who was going to be in control? Who was going to be in charge? Who was going to dominate what others think? It was all greed. This time greed had nothing to do with money, but power, control and influence of others. You may struggle with a strong desire in your heart to have influence over the minds and control over others, nevertheless it will have a disruptive effect on those who are around you. Greed to influence and control can destroy a unit, family and any group of people coming together to be on one-accord. Don't allow the need for power and influence to cause bitter envy and selfish ambition in your heart. If you truly want to be an influencer, God will not need you to be difficult, combative and argumentative to get the job done. You will influence and lead with wisdom, peace, consideration, submission, impartiality and good fruit. I will say, *"God is not the author of confusion, He is the author and finisher of our faith."* Therefore, if you are a Christian and are cantankerous, ferocious, argumentative and problematic, God is not the author of it. Don't let God set you up to be humbled like my brothers and sisters in Christ who served in the military service with me in Korea. I'm sure they never forgot that night as well. It makes one wonder after witnessing all the carnal behavior amongst our group if Mr. Hahn did not set this trip up on purpose to show the American's what a privilege they had to be born in a nation that could worship Christ freely and to see the remnants of an actual under-ground church that was hidden where people once risked their lives to do so.

Chapter Five

Greed in Relationships

"Who is wise and understanding among you? Let him show it by hi good life by deeds done in the humility that comes from wisdom. But if you harbor bitter envy and selfish ambition in your hearts, do not boast about it or deny the truth. Such "wisdom" does not come down from heaven but is earthly, unspiritual and of the devil. For where you have envy and selfish ambition, there you find disorder and every evil practice." James 3:13-16 (NIV)

Relationships are something that we all are a-part of whether many or few. It is in relationships that Satan does more damage in order to bring destruction through a Spirit of Greed. Ever since I was a young child, I have paid a lot of attention to relationships; especially between a man and a woman. By the time I was eight years old, I remember contemplating whether having a close relationship was worthwhile. What I saw in the lives of the older people around me was not good. I saw people unhappy, miserable, not in agreement, plenty of hurt and pain. I became afraid of the thought that one day that would happen to me if I ever was serious about someone in a relationship.

The thing I remembered most is the pain and divisiveness that I sensed that many people went through, who some I knew really loved each other. Now that I am older, I have had the privilege to experience that same dark side of relationships that I never really cared for when I was a kid. That being said, I think it is important to unveil what is the reason for so many frustrations in your relationships. I will discuss how the Spirit of Greed lurks in them and what the Word of God says about our relationships. The question the Apostle James put before the saints is: *"Who is **wise** and **understanding** among you? Let him show it by his good life by deeds done in the humility that comes from wisdom. But if you harbor bitter envy and selfish ambition in your hearts, do not boast about it or deny the truth. Such "wisdom" does not come down from heaven but earthly, unspiritual and of the devil. For where you have envy and selfish ambition, there you find disorder and every evil practice" James 3:13-14 (NIV).*

As I became a teenager, I began to be okay with dating. In my adult years, I have found that the areas Satan attacks mankind is in relationships through a Spirit of Greed. It is the hidden agendas, expectations, power plays, intense desires and unwillingness to share their lives fully with the person they are getting involved. Therefore, in order to get what they want, there is a lot of manipulation, control, deception and hesitation that goes on in friendships and dating arena. Why do we have so many dating agencies and dating websites in today's world? People are searching, but need help in finding the right person. They have had enough bad experiences and understand that they do not understand what people really want from them. They have failed in relationships time and time again, but can't seem to figure out why each relationship tends to turn out bad. There is a real reason and it has everything to do with how we operate in our relationships. It's called selfishness or Greed! To prove my point, let's look at greed in its definition, *"an intense and selfish desire for something, especially wealth or power."* You never know what people want out of your relationships, even if it's Pastoral. Relationships tend to have intense power struggles from either or both parties and when they do, failure, disappointment and destruction is not far away. The first thing we need to understand that it is Satan's job to conceal as much as possible about a person to another. This way he can use people's intense internal desires to bring destruction in the lives of others. Satan will never speak of his real motif operand. He is smart enough to keep them concealed until the proper time. We must realize that Satan's desire is to control the world and God's people. He wants to plant negative seed in your life so you would spend most of your time stumbling over personality issues, problems, difficulties, indifference and never focusing on what you should be doing for the kingdom of God and Christ. Think about it, how many couples you know spend years fighting each other and patching up the holes in their relationship rather than focusing on kingdom business. It's not *"kingdom"* for your relationships to be dysfunctional 300 out of 365 days a year. The negativity only comes to keep up the chaos, confusion and off the purpose and will of God for your life. You have to know that you are one that God has called and sent. The Apostle Paul wrote, *"And we know that in all things God works for the good of those who love him, who have been called according to his purpose" Romans 8:28.* And then there are those,*" who are created in Christ Jesus to do good works, which God has prepared in advance for them to do" Ephesians 2:1.*

The reason why Satan is able to bring so much chaos and confusion in our lives through relationships is written in scripture. *"But if you harbor bitter envy and selfish ambition in your hearts, do not boast about it or deny the truth. Such wisdom does not come down from heaven but is earthly, unspiritual and of the devil. For where you have envy and selfish ambition, there you find disorder and every evil practice" (James 3:14a).* The word *"harbor"* means to *shelter; refuge; hold in one's mind or conceal."* Selfish ambition is no less than greed. It is a spirit that has to be exposed in order to deal with it. Selfish ambition is normally well hidden by the person who is bound by it. This is the part of a persons' personality that Satan keeps concealed. We find out later what a person is really like in our relationships. This is a disadvantage for everyone. The Apostle James addressed the Church about bitter envy and selfish ambition because he saw that it was hindering the Christians from getting along with each other. The world that is bound by greed does not know that they are infected with selfish ambitions and intense desires, but the Apostle James wanted the church to be educated on the subject and steer away from it at all cost since it creates disorder and every evil practice.

Today, we commonly call it being "selfish or self-centered." Unfortunately, being selfish or self-centered, even though recognized by many, it is not given much thought in the minds of most men than it should. When a person appears to be self-centered, we typically label them as being a person that is *"selfish."* Many of us have learned to look at selfishness and ignore it as some temporary state of mind. Subconsciously, we think that selfishness is something that a person can grow out of or it can change at any in their life. Therefore, selfishness is something that most of us would disregard and minimize its real affects. Selfishness is much bigger than we think. It causes more damage than we are ready to face? Selfishness is not something you should ignore or minimize. Family, friendships, ministry, business and relationships can suffer from it severely.

What we don't realize is that selfishness or self-centeredness is not as temporary a state of mind. Self-centeredness is a strong-hold. It is a mind-set and a way of life for people who are bound by it. The older you get, the better you are at disguising it. Self-centeredness involves a lot of forethought, strategic planning and manipulation for the self-centered person. In the end, it is very destructive! Selfish people will drain your spirit and wear you out. Their whining, murmuring and complaining can be obsessive. It is their mission to remain in control and two steps ahead of you. By the time one may come close to figuring out what they are doing the damage is already done. Selfish folk also have an unbelievable imagination. They are constantly the victim in every situation. What they don't realize is that their problem lies within their own objectives for personal gain; which is Greed. They have an unrealistic imagination and short memory span. Unfortunately, you may not recognize this about them it right away. Putting on a mask in front of people is a common thing they do. The Apostle John warned us when he wrote *"Dear friends, do not believe every spirit, but test the spirits to see whether they are from God, (1 John 4:1).* The word of God teaches us about deceiving spirits. Unfortunately, we don't test every spirit like it tells us to do to see if it is from God or not. Regardless of any of our failures in the past, we have to take the Apostle's warning to heart. We desperately need to ask God for a *"spirit of discernment"* which is one of the nine gifts of the spirit in the bible *(1 Corinthians 12:8-10).* A *spirit of discernment* will help keep us from making many bad decisions concerning friendships and relationships that are dominated by selfish ambition. Anyone that has spent time around me knows that I am a real movie buff. I see things and get revelation out of movies that many don't see. That being said, I will talk about this one particular scene in a film I watched several years ago called *"Idle Wild."* This movie caught my attention and I learned some things from it. There was a particular scene when the well-known actor, Terrence Howard; was playing the role of a bad guy named *"Trumpy."* He was upset with one of his hit men for failing to do exactly what he told him and that was to follow a lady and not lose sight of her. The hit man failed at what *Trumpy* asked him to do and lost sight of her. When the hit man reported back to his boss – *Trumpy* and told him how he had lost sight of the girl, *Trumpy* quietly became upset. He grabbed his 38 revolver, emptied the chamber of the bullets, put one back in the chamber and spun it a few times. *Trumpy* began to make this statement to the hit-man while pointing the pistol at his right temple, *"In every relationship the person with the least amount of interest will control it."* Then he explained the reason why.

"Because person with the least amount of interest will always control it since they have no real reason to negotiate with you." Then he pulled the trigger at the hit man's head and luckily for him the revolver was sitting on one of the empty chambers. He did this to make a point to the hit man and everyone in the room that he was crazy, had no reason to negotiate with any of them and would kill them if he ever had to when they messed up. I was flabbergasted when this came across the film. This was a break through word for me and explained a lot I had been going through. I had been trying for years to get others to make a commitment whole-heartedly in the relationship just as much as I had to no avail. Every time I look up I was trying to figure out where I stood in the relationship. The problem is that they don't have the same interest or commitment to the relationship as you and have no real reason to negotiate. This is why things with them never go forward, but two steps backwards. In their mind, they have no reason to negotiate or work things out with you. The reality is that they are not all that committed in the first place. People negotiate and work out things with folk that they have an interest in. When I heard the actor, Terrence Howard, say these words it was like the lights came on for a lot that I had been dealing with for years. Unfortunately, some of your relationships will not value or appreciate you until many years later. Therefore, the next time you find yourself trying to figure out where you stand in a relationship with someone, maybe it's a signal to stop trying to figure out where you stand with them and start walking. Understand, selfishness is about control and is nothing less than Greed! This is why people that are bound by it feel that they can walk in and out of your life whenever they get good and ready. Some-times they feel like a nut, some-times they don't. Remember, it's a form of greed and not the person. They can at the flip of a switch threaten to walk out of your life and take everything that is important to you. Then turn around after they have a changed their mind and be cordial with you. This is sick and not kingdom at all. You have to get away from people like that if you are ever going to accomplish anything in your life. The threatening is more about controlling who you are. If you continue to get on this roller coaster ride with them, you will be harmed by their manipulative and spiritually inept behavior. I know that I am being candid, but it is paramount to inform you that your destiny in God is more important than chasing after someone that does not want to be caught. I leave you with a word that came out of the mouth of one of our nation's greatest preachers, Bishop TD Jakes; Potter's House; Dallas, Texas,

"When people can walk away from you, let them leave" I would say it like this, *"stop trying to hold on to people that don't want to stay and vacillate in and out of your life (alternate or waiver between two different opinions or actions; inconsistent) with*

you." Webster dictionary gives us a picture of what it means to be a vacillator. Vacillators *are sensitive and easily triggered by any hint of rejection or abandonment. They can feel easily overlooked, misunderstood or unloved. Over time, their passionate connection and intense good feelings of the early relationship are disturbed by anger, hurt and disappointment as "real life" sets in.* Making strong commitment to them can be costly. Be certain that every relationship you are involved in the two of you are fully invested and have a mutual interest in each other. Acknowledging these selfish traits early is critical. One thing that gives vacillators away is that they are constantly murmuring, complaining, uncooperative and inconsistent. Martyrdom is their middle name. Here is another quote I found in one of Bishop Thomas D. Jakes books worthy of attention: *"The martyr is the one who is always quick to say, "Oh poor me…" And fill in the blank. "If only I hadn't gotten pregnant so young I could have finished college." Translation: If I wasn't responsible for you kids I could have had a different life. "If only my mother hadn't been sick, I would have had the career I wanted." In other words: Because I was responsible for my mother there was no way I could go to school to train for the job I wanted. "If only I hadn't stayed married to your father, I would have been happier, but because my parents were divorced and it was so hard for me, I wanted you kids to have a mother and a father"* Bishop TD Jakes, Before You Do; pages 37-38.

People bound with selfish ambition can easily find fault with others in all their relationships. They can be very critical and cynical towards you. The bible calls them fault-finders. *"These people are grumblers and fault-finders; living only to satisfy their desires. They brag loudly about themselves, and they flatter others to get what they want (Jude 1:16)."* It pays to read your bible. They are very good at picking out another person's issue while satisfying them-self. They have terrible eyesight when it comes to looking at them-self and their own issues. Self-centeredness is a common problem in mankind. You have to understand that this spirit in relationships is not going to jump out of the closet and expose itself saying *"I'm full of greed and selfish ambition; everything has to go my way. I will plan, plot, covet and steal to see that it does."* Mind you, I was a lot like you. I didn't pay attention to how serious selfishness and self-centeredness impacting others really was until it was too late and impacted things in my life. Let me warn you, the spirit of Greed is real. Recognize it when it is in you and people who are very close to you. It is what our young people would say in today's world as being *"off the hook or off the chain."* It can be very lethal and destructive!

Here is a story I would like to tell you that helped me understand the destructive forces of selfish ambition. I was in a conversation with one of my very close older sister's in Christ that lives in Rochester, New York. We were sitting at her kitchen table one day when she began to share with me from her personal experience what happens in relationships between men and women. For the first time I would understand from a woman's perspective what is happening in a relationship when it starts to go wrong. As she began to talk, I didn't interrupt her because I knew I was finishing this chapter on *greed in relationships*, but she did not know it. I needed to hear what she had to say. I knew some things about her life and some of her experiences, but most of all, I knew her character and that she would not lie to me. She said something to me that caught my attention. She called the spirit out and let me know that the behavior she was referring to was *"self-centeredness."* She did not know, but it shook me when she said it. My sister in Christ had no idea that I was writing another book and was writing around this subject. I had been looking to gain more wisdom and insight on the matter in order to complete this chapter. I was totally fixed on what she was saying. I had been praying and saying to God, *"there is something I'm not mentioning so far in this book."* The bible say's *"The older women may teach the younger women" (Titus 2:4),* but this day, *the older woman taught the younger man,* and boy did it make sense. She is a spirit filled woman that knew what she was teaching me at her kitchen table from her experience. I gained plenty of understanding that day. What I needed to focus on for this chapter was *" self-centeredness. "* It was a destructive spirit and not a person, *"For we wrestle not against flesh and blood" (Ephesians 6:12).*

Self-centeredness is like an unpredictable storm. It will tear up relationships, friendships, families, teams and groups. It's a spirit that has been relegated in society because we don't understand how destructive it can be. Consider, when Hurricane Ike hit the Galveston and Houston, Texas area in Sept, 2008. Although it was recorded a category 2 storm, it was the initial thrust of the wide spread wind that did so much damage. It had the impact of a category four or five hurricane. All the experts unpredicted this storms fierce intensity. That is what self-centeredness is like. We can miscalculate or misjudge its intensity and power then are left looking at the aftermath of its destruction later. I watched a television reporter review of a mother and son who lived on the beach in Galveston, Texas and who had minimized how high the water would rise during Hurricane Ike. They refused to leave the area after being warned several times by police, city officials and emergency personnel.

This mother and son decided to stay with their property.

Several hours into the storm they began to rethink their decision. When they called 911 for help, the operator told them to write their social security numbers on their wrist so they can identify who they were after the storm. This was the reality of the serious trouble they were in. Fortunately, they both survived, but many of their neighbors that stayed and homes did not. They would go on national television to say that they would never minimize the intensity of a storm again. Likewise, that is what we need to understand about self-centered people that we keep in our lives and remain in relationship with them.

To ignore or down play the intensity of self-centeredness as a small storm that someone needs to get over and grow up can be a grave mistake. It's common to expect some high winds and not much damage from them. In truth, by the time it forces truly take affect; our homes are totally destroyed, buildings set on fire, fences are down, trees pulled up by the roots and power is down everywhere. Don't ever minimize the destructiveness of selfish ambition or self-centeredness in a person's heart that you are in marriage, relationship, friendship or in a business. The results can be devastating. The spirit of greed does not discriminate. Many of us in ministry are finding out that our own personal relationships have been impugned. We are learning that some of the people closest to us struggle with this spirit and it can have an impact on what we are doing for the kingdom of God.

The Holy Spirit said something to me several years ago that I never forgot while going through a very disappointing test and trial. I heard him say, *"Invest in things that have a return on you."* In other words, stop investing in people, things and relationships that refuse to give back a return. It totally liberated my way of thinking. A return can be something simple as appreciation, respect or a thank you. This revelation changed my life. I had to realize that any good business person looks at his bottom line - his return on investment (ROI). I never thought about that when dealing with relationships. Unfortunately, we as people spend 80% of our time investing in folk that refuse to return anything back to us. We spend more time wrestling and fighting with them. Likewise, 20% of our time is spent on the people who will give us a return on our investment in them. We have to flip the script. You have to start paying more attention to the people who appreciate, love and respect you and less time on those who do not. Why put yourself through so much stress? There is no need to sacrifice your-self in this way. Jesus was already the perfect sacrifice there is no need for another. This frame of mind will help us all get more done for ourselves and the Kingdom of God and Christ.

Millions of relationships, friendships and marriages suffer through the spirit of greed and selfish ambition. Love is not either being received or reciprocated. Marriage contracts do not make people love only a willing heart does. It is very possible to love a person and that love is not being given back.

Look at the life of Sampson who judged Israel for 20 years. Sampson fell in love with a prostitute named Delilah. When the Philistines saw that he loved her, each of the rulers of Gaza went to her and offered her 11,000 shekels each if she found out the secret to his strength and afforded them an opportunity to over-take him. In the book of Judges 16:4 -5, it reads: " *Some-time later, he fell in love with a woman in the Valley of Sorek whose name was Delilah. The rulers of the Philistines went to her and said, "See if you can lure him into showing you the secret of his great strength and how we can overpower him so we may tie him up and subdue him. Each one of us will give you eleven hundred shekels of silver."*

Delilah, doing what a prostitutes does, greedy for ill-gotten gain, consented and in time found out the secret to Sampson's strength. She sold him out to his Philistine enemies. Wait a minute – I thought Sampson was in love? Absolutely! It doesn't matter; she was in greed and sold him out. What we don't really understand is that there were five rulers over Gaza that was interested in Sampson's capture. Each one giving her 11,000 shekels added up to be 55,000 shekels. In truth, Delilah knew that she would never have to *"turn a trick again" (meaning never having to prostitute again in life)* if she cooperated with the rulers. Delilah knew she would be financially set for life. Unfortunately, in this love story the bible says' that Sampson fell in love with Delilah. The bible never said Delilah fell in love with him; therefore she had no reason to negotiate with the Philistines about not taking Sampson's life. Here is where I want to make a point to you. In relationships, friendships and marriage *"make sure that the person that you are in love with also is fully in love with you."* If not, you are going to have nightmares. Real love is reciprocal. It doesn't change like the weather. A person that really loves you loves you unconditionally. A person who doesn't understand this can love you today and hate you tomorrow. They are like *"shifting shadows."* That will never make for a good marriage, relationship, or friendship. Sampson and Delilah's relationship was lop-sided from the beginning that is why she could sell him out to the Philistines without a conscience.

My encouragement to you is to deal with the facts and evaluate the relationships that you have in your life, all of them! Be willing to call a mistake a mistake and don't waste your love and time in the wrong place. Take note of the relationships that you enjoy that are easy to be in and adds value to your life. Create space on the one's that causes you so much work, pain and heart-ache. You must realize the many years that you have wasted with their selfishness. Don't be afraid to bring each one of your relationships into account for their lack of interest in the relationship and move on. Nevertheless, beware of their excuses of why they behave the way they do. They will have plenty of them, old and new ones. Don't fall for it. The real reason is that they are self-centered, self-absorbed and not willing to share their world, life and heart with yours. No one that cares about you will have issue with you for 48 out of a 52 week calendar year.

Lastly, many of our selfish relationships are about control. Who's going to be in control? Who's going to run the show? What we do not understand is that the person who wants to dominate the relationship has no intentions on cooperating with you anyway. That is a good word for us to focus on "Co-operate." If you look at it the first part of the word "Co" which means: *joint, mutual or common*. The second part of the word is "Operate" which means: *control the functioning of (a machine, process or system)*. Therefore, a couple that has "co-operation" you will find joint/mutual/common functioning of the relationship together. There is no room for greed or selfish ambition. The person filled with greed will not want to release the contention for they fear that they would lose the control over the situation. They are controlling you through their issues, anger, attitudes and frustration while not allowing there to be a resolution. Their greed for control comes from their need for power and to combat their low self-esteem. That's not love - its childishness! Many children act this way. They feel the need to take control of their lives by rebelling against authority, their parents and teachers. Regardless of what happens, they will not *"cooperate."* The game is to resist and rebel as much as possible in order to feel in control of their situation. This stems from immaturity and selfish ambition. Unfortunately, they are setting themselves up for a difficult life ahead. They will reap the harvest of the seeds they have sown and will not be able to ignore later. If you are a person that you can see you are bound with the spirit of greed in your relationships, you are withholding love, joy and peace through selfish ambition. Bitterness has you by the collar and you refuse to exemplify genuine love, thankfulness, respect and appreciation for the one that love you. I say to you *"come out of yourself"* and become the person that God wants you to be. You will never have success in your relationships and continue to cause pain, heartache, disappointment and grief in everyone that gets close to you. End your self-centered world and be free of the spirit of greed!

Chapter Six
Greed in Raising Children

The Lord abhors dishonest scales, but accurate weight is his delight (Proverbs 11:1)

This will be one of the toughest but most important subjects that I will write about in this book concerning the Spirit of Greed. Before I do, let me make each of you aware that I have committed myself to use what I consider to be a qualified litmus test on every book that I write henceforth before releasing them to the general public. After writing my first book ***"CHOOSE,"*** I sent a copy of the book to a dear family member who was serving time in Kentucky at a Federal Prison called *"Big Sandy."* I would later find out that the one copy I sent to my family member also was read by his cellmate and then it went around to many inmates on his cell block. The general response was that the book had touched the lives of many inmates because it was straight to the point, very matter of fact, not theological, written to where everyone could understand it. In other words, the inmates could hear it, understand it and receive it. I was told that several inmates had torn out the page(s) from the book and plastered them on the walls in their cells. It was reported back to me they had kept the page(s) that had ministered directly to them as spiritual information if they had known early in their life they would have never been in prison. It was an unexpected response. What an unusual honor I felt when I heard these things. I had only expected to send my loved one their copy of my first book and that was it, but it ended up reaching multiple men in the cell block.

That day, I realized that I never want to write a book that a man or woman sitting in a prison cell could not relate to. Inmates became my heart and my first priority in communication and people I wanted to reach. If there is one thing I know about those in prison is that you can't sugar coat the Word with them, they are already doing difficult time. They have heard and seen it all because they have lived it. They know when you are full of it and when you are not. They have plenty of time on their hands to read, think, reflect and decipher anyone's writings. What I write on this subject on the *"Spirit of Greed in Raising Children,"* know that many in prison will read it first before some of you may get upset in what I say in this chapter. I will keep that in mind in all my writings. I know the things that I will talk about in this chapter will hit home. Let us begin.

Firstly, I want to say that we all are aware that not all kids are brought up in a single parent home. Many kids are brought up in homes with two parents or guardians. The term family in modern America is constantly changing and can exist with any number of relatives, friends or acquaintances that provide for the morale and welfare of a child. What I want to address is the traditional or the biblically written definition a family is to exist in the world and that is children having the leadership and guidance of a *mother* and *father.* To this definition and this definition only will I be addressing so there is no confusion as to whom and what I am talking about. The reason why I am doing this is because much of what I will be referencing and sharing insight on is coming from the bible. If you looked at the scripture at the beginning of this chapter, it say's *"The Lord abhors dishonest scales, but accurate weights are his delight."(Proverbs 11:1).* I want you to think about this verse in terms of children having a mother and a father. God doesn't like anything that is out of balance. I don't know about you, but I have read this scripture many times over the years and never really understood why it was written in the bible. I want to share with each of you why this verse is revealed in scripture about the Lord. It is simply written to give us another piece of insight into the Lord's personality. We must understand this about God. The Lord likes balance. He does not like unfairness, cruelty or anything unjust. In fact, according to this scripture, He hates or abhors it! *"The Lord abhors dishonest scales" (Proverbs 11:1).*

There is an interesting story in the book of Exodus that reveals how God feels about unfairness or what is unjust. The cruel oppression of the Egyptians towards the Israelites had them in intense slavery for 400 years? God heard their cry and the call of the Israelites. Even though this was a prophecy to Abram from God that this would happen to his people – God still didn't like how they were being treated and committed Him-self to bring them out with a mighty hand. Isn't it amazing how God choose the most cruel, unjust and unfair act of slavery to show the world His strength and power? In fact, when God heard the cries of the Israelites in Egypt he looked for a man, Moses, and he said to him *"I have indeed seen the misery of my people in Egypt, I have heard them crying out because of their slave drivers, and I am concerned about their suffering. So I have come down to rescue them from the hand of the Egyptians and to bring them up out of that land into a good and spacious land, a land flowing with milk and honey" (Exodus 3:7-9).* Three key words in this verse that I need you to concentrate on is that God *seen, heard* and *came.* The systemic punishment of slavery was so cruel in God's eyes and ears that He was willing to *"come down"* from heaven (It moved Him off His Throne) and speak to Moses to send him to His people to let them know that help was on the way. Why? Because He had seen, He had heard, therefore; He will come! That was then, this is now.

One of the cruelest, meanest, unfair, unjust practices in modern times I have watched for many years is the evil intent of adults keeping their children from having a relationship with their other parent (mom or dad). This has got to be the most selfish, immature and satanic practice I have witnessed. People psychologically, mentally, emotionally, spiritually, physically and systematically causing dissension between the children and the other parent is not only greed but it is evil. I have met those who would go as far as calling this form of manipulation outright *"witchcraft."* Bound with anger, hatred, bitterness, and jealously they camouflage what they are doing as protecting their children. Don't get me wrong, some kids need to be shielded and protected from certain parents who are very abusive and destructive. If you don't believe me, read the book by Debra Ann Brown-Davis *"My Daddy the Devil and Me."* But this foolishness that I am talking about is destroying the morale, spirit, soul and minds of our kids. I know this is hard statement, but it happens every day. Unfortunately, like God, I have seen this epidemic in people who make it appear like they are taking precautions on the behalf of their children, but in reality; they are deceptive, abusive and sowing discord.

The real reason is in response to the hidden anger that is within their hearts towards the other parent. Like God; I heard the cry of the children and am concerned about their suffering. Therefore, I have come forth to write about it and not *"sugar coat it"* for anyone. It is abusive and wrong! This too is a form of a Spirit of Greed in people who want to single handedly or selfishly have sole control, influence and voice in their children's life. I have seen too many incidents of this since I was a young boy, so many angry men and women who do this to their children and try to cover it up to make it look like they are great mom or dad, but will not consider what they are doing to their child. I do not claim to know everything, but what I do know and have seen, I have no problem in talking about it. This mess has got to stop! It is killing our children self-esteem and confidence from one generation to the next.

Children have been growing up for many years in a lopsided society particularly knowing only one parent and one side of their family. They have been treated as if they are property and a half a person. This has been epidemic in our communities for a very long time and we must shine the light upon it and call it what it is. Our kids are losing out on a balance of direction for their lives and being left to figure life out on their own. The vilest part about this spirit is that many parents are going to the extreme measure of brainwashing their children to not want anything to do with their other parent. This is where I agree with those who may call it *"witchcraft."* To me, any form of brainwashing is *"witchcraft."* If you are doing it, then you are a witch! There are male witches called – *warlocks* and there are female witches, so don't think I am just talking about women since I am a man. I have seen it in both genders. When this happens it causes a very difficult situation for kids. The children have to choose between their parents which is called *"sowing discord"* (another thing that God hates) *"There are six things the Lord hates, seven that are detestable to him; haughty eyes, a lying tongue, hands that shed innocent blood, a heart that devises wicked schemes, feet that are quick to rush into evil, a false witness who pours out lies and a person who sows discord (Proverbs 6:16-19)*. Because of this discord sown, children feel empowered to resist and rebel against the other parent's authority and begin to take confidence in the parent that perpetrates the division. In the end, the child begins to take on character and behaviors that are unlike themselves and for a-while lose sight of and direction for their life. Fortunately, some of these children realize later that this was not wise to participate in. By the time they may realize it, they can find themselves behind in day to day living experiences that they need in order to advance their lives. In other words, they can feel like they are playing catch-up with those who were never derailed in this fashion. Although it is possible for the child to get back on course and move forward, the reality is that it can be a struggle for them to do so. To be honest, this is not cute, right, profitable or justifiable. It hurts our kids. Too many offending parents get children caught up in their adult affairs. Again, this is hurting children mentally, spiritually, psychologically and emotionally. No child should be put in the middle of adult problems and suffer from this sort of psychological manipulation from any parent.

The Spirit of Greed in parenting has been at large for centuries. Parents have swindled, bamboozled and abused children into thinking that they don't need the other parent in their life. They discretely convince them that they can do it all by themselves and do not need to listen to or respect the other parents advise, opinion or counsel. The reason they do this is because most of them have been raised, manipulated and treated this way by their own parent. It keeps passing down from generation to generation. At the end of the day, children are growing up in families without the emotional, spiritual and psychological balance of influence from mom and dad, which brings balance. To say it, but this is not pleasing to our courts, but there is very little they can do about it. How often our judges and lawyers see this disease in court room's everyday? The bible teaches kids, *"Children, obey your parents in the Lord, for this is right. Honor your father and mother – which is the first commandment with a promise. That it may go well with you and that you may enjoy long life in the earth" Ephesians 6:1- 3*. Notice that it didn't say *"Children, obey your parent"*, nor did it say, *"Only honor your father or mother."* Recognize, when we teach our children to NOT obey their parents, then we teach them to do differently from the word of God and confuse them. Not only that, we take away their future promise of *"life going well for them and having long life."* Our children's obedience to both parents is tied to their first commandment that has this promise attached to it; no child can get around it. *"That it may go well with you and that you may enjoy long life in the earth"*. All of our kids need this promise to come to fruition in their lives from God. Unfortunately, many parents are putting their hands on that promise for our children before they can get started by aiding and abetting them in their rebellion toward the other parent through their own selfish greed and ambition. You may ask me how? *When you as a parent have said things to your children to make them think and feel that the other parent is bad news, then your mouth is the weapon that Satan uses to cause discord and un-forgiveness in the children's heart towards the other parent that should have never been there.* May I say this to any offending parents - the promise is not for you, but for the kids! Learn to honor your own father and mother and inherit your own blessings and stop robbing your children from getting all of theirs.

If greed was not a real factor in parenting, then; why is it that so many kids grow up only knowing one of their parents? Why do many not have a good relationship with both sides of their family? I am not talking about moms' or dads' who do not show any effort in having a relationship with the children they make. That's another book. Not all children are growing up with one of their parents deceased. There can be good reasons why a child is growing up with one parent, but in our world, it seems to be countless excuses for one parent to be controlling and have sole voice for the upbringing of the children. This has been one of Satan's secret under handed weapons that he has been using to control the world and destroy children future.

What I am trying to say is that many children in the world know both parents, but there is one side of that child's life that the children never really gets to know, especially in their early development. Why is this? Could it be that the spirit of greed has crept into our homes in the raising of children? I'll let you think about that for a minute. Listen, it is common sense that children need a balance as to who they are whether they realize it or not. Kids are not possessions or half of people, but a whole person that is made up of two people, not one. Unfortunately, the greed in America, even with our children is causing them to grow up with severe identity crisis. They are struggling on the inside as to who they really are because they are only identifying with half of their deoxyribonucleic acid (DNA). This subject is very close to me for I grew up in a single mother's home. My late mother did a wonderful job raising me, my two older brothers and little sister. We all love and respect her to this day for what she did for us as a single parent. But I have to tell you, I am so glad that my mother orchestrated an opportunity for me and my siblings to meet our father. It balanced out so much for me as to who I am as a man. I was a senior in high school a football, basketball and track athlete and was enlisting in the United States Air Force. She set up a time for my father to meet me for lunch the same day I was taking the oath to serve in the United States Air Force. It was a very strange day, but at the same time it was a new day for me. For all intense and purpose, my upbringing and training was over, but I still needed coaching *(For details, order my book "Everybody Needs A Coach")*. I was starting my adulthood. Let me tell you, even that late in my youth, meeting my father was a great blessing in my life. My father brought in a level of coaching and understanding in my life that was very instrumental. I was able to get to know him and his side of the family. Immediately, it became much clearer who I was as a whole person. It answered so many questions I had as a child and gave me *"balance."* More importantly, it gave me confidence in who I was, cleared up any identity issues and validated my personality as a young man. I didn't have to make any excuses. I knew fully who I was not long after developing a relationship with him. I was a lot like my dad! My mother and father's break up was their business, not mine. I got to hang out with him and get to know him for the next twelve years and then dad past away of cancer. He and I became Father and Son, the best of friends and my parents both got to share in the influence of my life, education and military career. The question I have for you is - will a parent conspire to have more control and influence on the raising the kids then than the other? The spirit of greed has been lurking in our homes even when it comes to parenting, influencing and raising our children. I can't begin to tell you how many kids I grew up with that did not know or have a relationship with their father. This is a huge problem in our society and it has a lot to do with so much crime in America. All communities deal with this issue, some more than others. The cycle is vicious and it never ends. Countless children and adults go about every-day life trying to figure out who they are in this world with identity issues, only knowing half of who they really are.

I heard a story where a prison ministry would provide material for the male inmates to make cards for their mother's during *"Mother's Day"* and almost every inmate participated and made cards with joy for their mothers and sent them out. That same prison ministry a month later provided the same opportunity for these inmates to make cards for their father's and almost no one accepted the material. Man, if that is not enough to make you say *"Wow!"* Why does this happen? Who is doing this and why? We'll if we are biblically well inform we know that it is Satan who is doing this in our communities.

The vehicle that he is using is through a diabolical spirit of greed through the lack of knowledge in parenting and leadership over the children. The Prophet Hosea said: *"My people are destroyed for the lack of knowledge (Hosea 4:6)."* Psychologists have been studying this epidemic for many years. In fact, most lower class and middle class Americans don't know of it or ever heard of it. Psychologist will tell you that it does exist, but very difficult to prove in court. Judges and Lawyers are well aware of its existence. The spirit that I am referring to is called *"Parental Alienation Syndrome (PAS)."* The lack of knowledge about *"PAS"* and the affects that it has on our children has become a stronghold in our homes and communities. Let's talk a little about PAS, you can do research by using Google or Wikipedia on your own to learn more. I know it may be a term that you may or may not be familiar with but by the time I finish this chapter you will have a general idea of what it is and understand why I am referring to it as a *"Spirit of Greed in Raising Children."* This is what one parent does when they desiring to have the majority, if not sole influence over their children. PAS is a syndrome that many Psychologist and mental health specialist have found in children of divorced parents. The key word is *"alienation."* These children are alienated from a parent by the manipulation and brainwashing of the other. One writer describes PAS as *"disturbance occurring in children who are preoccupied with depreciation and criticism of a parent and denigration that is unjustified and/or exaggerated.* He describes these children *"obsessed with hatred of a parent."* Many children growing up today without a father or mother are also experiencing these same feelings of alienation. The feeling of why my other parent has not come around to see about me. What that child does not know is the parents desire to be there, but anger from the manipulating parent is preventing it from happening. The subject of Parental Alienation Syndrome is very real. In fact; I would like to list several criteria that mental health professionals have found with alienating parents and children who have been affected by PAS:

Child is preoccupied with depreciation and criticism of the parent that is unjustified and/or exaggerated.

Conscious, subconscious, and unconscious factors within the alienating parent contribute to the child's alienation from the other.

Denigration of the parent has the quality of a litany, a rehearsed quality. There is phraseology not usually used by the child.

Child justifies the alienation with memories of minor

altercations experienced in relationship with the parent which are trivial and which most children would have forgotten. When asked, the children are unable to give more compelling reasons.

The alienating parent will concur with the children and support their belief that these reasons justify the alienation. Hatred of the parent is most incense when the alienating parent and the child are in the presence of the alienated parent. However, when the child is alone with the alienated parent, the child may exhibit hatred, neutrality, or expressions of affection.

If the child begins to enjoy him/herself with the alienated parent, there may be episodes of "stiffening up" and resuming withdrawal and animosity, as though they have done something wrong. Alternatively, the child may ask the alienated parent not to reveal his/her affection to the other parent.

The degree of animosity in the child's behavior and verbalizations may vary with the degree of proximity to the alienating parent.

Hatred of the parent often extends to include alienated parent's extended family, with even less justification by the child.

The alienating parent is generally unconcerned with the psychological effects on the child of the rejection of parent and extended family.

The child's hatred of the alienated parent is often impervious to evidence which contradicts his/her position.

The child's position seemingly lacks ambivalence. The

alienated parent is "all bad," the alienating parent is "all good."

The child is apt to exhibit a guiltless disregard for the feelings of the alienated parent.

The child fears the loss of the love of the alienating parent.

See *"The Parental Alienation Syndrome: An analysis of sixteen cases"* by John Dunne and Marsha Hedrick

(http://www.fact.on.ca/Info/pas/dunne.htm)

Why is this important? Many people are extreme alienators with children and they are bound by a spirit of greed to parent and have ultimate influence on the child's life. By the time the offending parent recognizes that what he/she is doing is wrong, the damage is severe to the child or children.

Several years ago, I met a young man in his early 40's at a men's prayer meeting which encompassed everything I just wrote about. He was a victim of PAS and did not know it at the time. He and I talked in depth on several occasions. In fact, he described it as *"having an unhealthy emotional relationship with his mother and grandmother, yet without sex."* He told me how he looks back and sees how it impaired his relationship not only with his father, but with other men. He even recognized how it caused problems in his life in his marriage. He told me that he struggled in having a proper relationship with another woman outside of his mother and grandmother who dominated his belief system and up-bringing. I don't know who this is for, but somebody reading, this chapter, it is for you or somebody that you know. Majority of the time, the child doesn't even know that they suffer from this, but they know something is wrong within them. This is one of the most silent and destructive forms of abuse that is going on in our society today. The moment that you bring it up to the alienator, it is clearly denied and attack. The sad part of this is that many doctors, lawyers, and judges know that this (PAS) exist, but it is one of the hardest arguments to prove in court, and is often thrown out since it is so vehemently denied by the offending parent. In fact, most courts have found the only cure for it is to move the child/children completely out of the offending parent's home since it's the behavior of the parent they can't control. Most courts do not want to move the children completely out of any parents home unless it is physical abuse. Although this is abuse, it is abuse of another kind. It is more mental, emotional and psychological abuse.

Lastly, our state legislators (law makers) in the past have been a big part of the parental alienation syndrome that has impacted so many children I will explain why. Understand that the savvy politicians that design laws and perpetuate the low income parent to depend on the social welfare system for themselves and their children know that a *"fatherless"* child is more than likely to live in a vicious cycle that weakens his/her opportunities of obtaining real success. In other words, her children are more than likely to remain poor. Even though these politicians know that they can control a certain class of people, many of them still rise up under these conditions. Crafty legislators establish these systems while at the same time having the power to make the policy for women to qualify for its benefits for her and her children. One of the rules is to make sure that she has no male adult living at her residence while she receives benefits. The home has to be fatherless. But who is really benefiting? Are these families really benefiting and learning at an early age how to become self-sufficient and independent? The problem is that many of these families get tired of living in lack and therefore don't have any faith in the world system. The results are crime, violence and people looking to get what they feel is theirs at any cost. It's a warped way of thinking, but it is the reality of the financially and parentally unbalanced. Many of these children are raised fatherless. In order for these women to continue to receive their benefits, there can be no father in the home. So what happens? The government has established a system that makes our women choose money over what's really needed for our children. Many women become dependent on a system that is not designed to prosper her and the children, but ultimately keep them struggling. She ignores the need for balance in the child's life for the reality of the need for food on her table and a roof over her kids head. We have to fix this! Furthermore, there are too many men and women out here having babies just for child support or more welfare benefits in their pay checks. This is nothing more than a "spirit of greed in parenting." We have to truly think about why we are having kids and stop using them to fill voids in our life that no one can fill but God and his Word.

Therefore, if a child is psychologically, emotionally, spiritually, or physically brain-washed or manipulated about his/ her mother or father, then that child will grow up as an adult void of his/her full identity. He/She will suffer like symptoms that I mentioned the young man I met a few years ago. The spirit of greed in parenting and the social welfare systems have promoted a real problem for many children. Children need an accurate weight of relationship from both parents when being developed. For too long it's been a one sided influence on the raising of kids. Most of the parenting and influencing in America has been done by one parent. Our kids need balance, a just weight. It is time for this to stop and those who would have an ear to hear be educated on the subject of PAS. If it doesn't, the cycle will continue turn and create under developed, inexperienced children will continue walk into adulthood unprepared to deal with real life. Let's get rid of the Spirit of Greed in our parenting and start treating our children as a whole person and ensure that they have a balanced relationship with both parents in these last and difficult days.

Chapter Seven

Greed in Marriage

"And Abraham called the name of the place, Jehovah-Jireh; as it is said to this today. "The mount of the Lord it shall be provided." Genesis 22:14

I guess one would ask; what does the spirit of Greed have to do with marriage? Well, you would be surprised in what I have noticed in marriages that have the elements of greed. If you think about it, many times when a marriage goes bad, you can normally trace the roots to financial needs, issues and problems. I always found that interesting because when two people say their vows to one another in the presence of witnesses, they pledge to stay together *"for better or worse, for richer or poorer."* Now I don't know about you, but it seems to me that that declaration need not be read by the minister because very few people mean it when they say it. Their actions speak louder than their words. I can't tell you the amount of marriages I have seen break up when the money is tight. In fact, many women are very open today about how their spouse has to be able to do so much for them financially if they are going to be with them. This attitude puts a lot of pressure on their husbands and stress on the marriage. On the other hand we have people admitting that they married a person because they had money, or the next time they marry it will be for money, but the money couldn't keep them together. So what do you say we have here? We have a big mess in marriages and greed is right in the middle of it. The unfortunate thing about the dynamics of money or wealth in a marriage is that if you are bound by greed, there are still going to be many occasions that you or your spouse is going to express dissatisfaction on what they do or do not have. It's a very difficult thing for anyone to have to go through. As a man, I know that women want security. I also know that when all the needs are met in her mind that you have a more pleasant environment at home. Also, I have lived long enough to know that when there is lack in the home, the man can forget about having a peaceful environment to lay his head. He can forget about pleasant place to bring their needs to the Lord in order for Him to show him the way out. What that being said, women or men who marry for money must understand from the on-set that their spouse is not *"Jehovah Jireh,"* that is His name - only the Lord can be that to them. A good reminder for all marriages when there is a need is found in Philippians 4:6 - *"Do not be anxious about anything, but in every situation, by prayer and petition, with thanksgiving, make your request to God."* In other words, there must be an element of faith exemplified in all marriages that trust God through all seasons. This is why the wedding vows states *"for better and for worse."* Obviously, Job's wife did not understand this when she asked him *"Are you still maintaining your integrity? Curse God and die* (Job 2:9)! How hypocritical it is when we can shout the victory during the good times, but can't believe God during the trying times. Unfortunately, many are anxious and fearful and look for the first excuse to jump ship when the heat is on financially in the marriage. I know that my book is not user friendly, but hang with me for your break through. The fact is that what I am writing about, very few men would ever have the heart to say to their wives. This tells me that men know money is extremely important to their women. What a man needs to understand that it may not be you who she is in love with, it can be your financial ability to take care of her that she loves more, only trying times can reveal that to you. Job found out the hard way. If that is the case, a financial setback will put your marriage in a tail spin. Marriage is about covenant, richer or poorer. Those who honor their covenant and love each other, survive financial set-backs of any kind time and time again.

So the question is *"at what expense do we go after money?"* I have been spending many of my middle age years trying to understand people and money. I have found that we all want it, but very few of us knows how to get it and don't have patience for those who are trying to find out. I have also found that many who get it become dependent on it and become jerks when they get it. So where is the balance? Where is the just weight? How do you provide for your family but don't lose your mind in doing so? How can you have high seasons and rejoice with your love ones and then hit a low seasons and still know that they are always there for you and you are in it together, *until death do us part?* If you look at the statistics, its money that is undoing marriages part more than death. Over 50 percent of first time marriages end in divorce. Over 60 percent of second time marriages end this way and over 72 percent of third time marriages are ending in divorce. Need I say more? The issue is that we don't see too many marriages staying together through financial crisis. Couples today don't know how to stay off each other's back when the money or economy is low. Likewise, there are many that don't know how to stay out of the drug house and the whore house when the money is good. We don't know how to be abased and abound. I got news for you. Christian marriages are not exempt from experiencing more than enough and need.

To be honest with you, we are instructed in the word of God so that we can be the examples to the world in both conditions. Let's look with Paul said *"I know both how to be abased, and I know how to abound: every-where and in all things I am instructed both to be full and to be hungry, both to abound and to suffer need"* (Philippians 4:12.)

If this is the word of God, and the Apostle said this himself, then why is it in Christian homes we see the opposite. Why are Christians getting married and not realizing that they are going to have highs and lows and it's not worth fighting and losing your marriage and family over it? It's as though we want to be Christians, but we want the world's mentality when it comes to wealth when it comes to our marriages. What I want to say is, if you are not willing to put up with highs and lows in your finances in a marriage as a Christian, then you need to decide if you want to marry someone that is going to keep you well off and stop using the title *"Christian"* and use the right one *"Greedy."* The last I looked in my bible, Christians are over comers. They are not surprised about the lows and know that they will rise again. Believers know that trouble don't last always and focuses on getting through the storm and not fighting the one that is *"bone of their bones and flesh of their flesh (Genesis 2:23)"* Think about it. If you and your spouse or fiancée were on a cruise ship and it went down. Let's say, somehow you and your spouse survived and got in a life boat. Now remind you that you are out in the open sea with nothing or no one around. The storm comes again and begins to beat against your little boat. What good does it do if you start yelling at your spouse about the winds and the waves crashing against the life boat? Is that going to get the two of you out of the situation? No! What good is it going to do if you decide to save yourself, jump out of the boat and swim to safety? Did you really save yourself, or did the sharks come and get you first?

My point is that when a marriage begins to experience turbulence or financial set-backs and your spouse is works it out with you, that is when you know that you have a good marriage partner. I don't get people today. It's all about them and not the family. They say they love you, but mess around and have a financial set back and you will see just how much they love you. Let a business deal not go bad and you will see how much they love you. Let another person come in their life that seems more promising financially and you will see how much they love you. Let an unexpected financial obligation you have to pay come in and you will see how much they love you. God forbid that you get laid off or fired and they will go another direction. Why does this happen? Because many people love what you do for them and very few has learned to love you. Let's not lie anymore to the preachers or judges and say *"until death do us part"* when we don't mean it. Let's be honest and say according to statistics *"until money do us part."*

On the other hand, I have seen the strangest thing, woman who husbands or boyfriends who are in prison, visit and stay with those men during their entire term. It is clear that these men cannot provide financially for their families while in jail. Yet, many of these ladies stay with them and faithfully visit on a regular basis. It doesn't matter if you and I agree, but it still happens. Then we have those at home who if their spouse is short on a car payment, they are ready to go live with their mother. I mean it doesn't make sense. Some where there has to be a balance. The way I see it, if I am married, and my wife goes to jail, she is still my wife. I need to see to it that she has what she needs while she serves her time. If she is stricken with a disease and has to remain in the hospital, she is still my wife. If she sleeps with another man, then she is not my wife. If she doesn't want to be married anymore, then she is not my wife. The point I'm trying to get us to see is that your spouse is your spouse regardless of the financial situation you are in. You need to honor your marriage and stop showing your spouse that you only love them for what they can do for you. People are not cars or trucks. You don't trade up just because you don't want to drive it anymore or it's getting a little less mileage. Marriage is a covenant - it is not a football try out. Since there is so much greed in marriages in our society what we have is a bunch of *"covenant breakers"* in the home. They marry and if you make the mad or don't meet their needs they shut down and are out. I say if they want to go, let them go. In fact, the Word of God teaches you to do so.

The Apostle Paul said it this way to the church in Corinth. He said *"To the married I give this command (not I, but the Lord): A wife must not separate from her husband. But if she does, she must remain unmarried or else be reconciled to her husband. And a husband must not divorce his wife. To the rest I say this (I, not the Lord): If any brother has a wife who is not a believer and she is willing to live with him, he must not divorce her. And if a woman has a husband who is not a believer and he is willing to live with her, she must not divorce him. The unbelieving husband has been sanctified through his wife and the unbelieving wife has been sanctified through her believing husband. Otherwise your children would be unclean, but as it is, they are holy.* **But if the unbeliever leaves, let him do so. A believing man or woman is not bound in such circumstances; God has called us to live in peace" (1 Corinthians 7:10-15).** I like what Paul say's about the unbelieving spouse that leaves or wants to leave. *"Let them go."* Believers have to learn to stop trying to hold on to someone who behavior shows them that they don't want to be there. It doesn't matter if they say they are Christian, their behavior is saying something else. Believers don't break their marriage covenant, but Christians do. I will let you think about that for a moment. We must understand that believers don't act this way, they keep their covenant, therefore don't get twisted or confused if a person who is a Christian begins to behave in a way that is like an unbeliever. Let them go! Free yourself from the marriage contract and live in peace. Above all, the Lord encourages us all to remain with our spouses whether they are believers or not if their desire is to remain married to you. Love them and be good to them, they are your spouse. Don't allow greed or need to cause you to look to leave your husband or wife just because you are in a bad financial season. The Lord is Jehovah-Jireh. He is your provider. Only He can meet your needs and is in full support of your marriage covenant.

Chapter Eight
Greed in the lyrics of Music

"This is what you are commanded to do, O peoples, nations and men of every language: As soon as you hear the sound of the horn, flute, zither, lyre, harp, pipes and all kinds of music, you must fall down and worship" Daniel 3:4-5

If what I have written about so far has not caused you to think about greed in a different way, then I know this chapter will definitely help you to do so. I am going to talk to you about the spirit of greed that is in music. That's right, the music. Just turn on any secular radio station or television program and listen for a-while. We all can hear what's going on. The younger generation all over the country running after the almighty dollar, drugs, sex and violence and its being promoted through music and videos, just another form of greed that has gone viral. Unfortunately, these young people are not old enough to have heard the song *"Money-Money-Money-Money"* made in the 1970's by the O Jay's. The Hip-Hop genre has changed so much since the 70s & 80s and has gotten worse since the 1990s. The young generation has lost their minds over material gain.

They can't have enough, get enough and will do anything to get what they want. Many want to be a star right now without putting in the work or patience to get there. Our television programs promote it and tell the kids that it is who they want to be to the point that they are letting go education, training and a relationship with God. When I was in the USAF Presidential Honor Guard and living in the Maryland/Washington D.C area in 1987, I remember a long article that was in the Washington Post that there was on average $10,000 worth of jewelry that could be collected from the kids in per classroom in a high school in Anacostia, Virginia. I remember teenagers dying in that area and South-East DC at an alarming rate behind guns, drugs and violence. Unfortunately, one of them was University of Maryland basketball star Lenny Bias behind a cocaine over dose less than 24 hours after signing a Million Dollar contract with the World NBA Champions – Boston Celtics and later his younger brother Jay Bias after an apparent ambush by two gunmen after an argument and while driving out of the Prince George's Plaza shopping center. In fact, in the mid-1980s, there was a statistical report in the news that the average young black male in the Washington DC area would not live much past their 21st birthday. It was very bad and it got my attention. I was 25 years of age myself and was in the military working daily in the District of Washington, DC. It was so deplorable that the Army National Guard was patrolling some of the streets in Washington, DC. Prince George County was seeing murders at an alarming rate. Trust me when I say that in that area, there was no such thing as a *"broke drug dealer."* I saw it with my own eyes, these young boys ages 15, 16 and 17 years old were making crazy money and driving Jaguars, Mercedes Benz, BMWs, Ninja Motorcycles…etc. They had the gold, the money and the girls.

These kids had sold their souls to the enemy in the 1980's to get money as fast and as much as they could. In fact, the drug King Pin in the Washington area *"Rayful Edmonds"* (who many still believe was betrayed by the government to protect many powerful politicians on Capital Hill) was arrested on racketing charges and only 22 years of age himself at the time. Rayful Edmonds was considered the *"True King of Cocaine. At his peak he sold 2,000 kilos a week, reaped gross profits of $70 million dollars a month, and ran an operation with over 150 soldiers to support him. In his life champagne flowed like water. Trips to Vegas, New York and Los Angeles were the norm and $150,000 shopping sprees were nothing. He was responsible for distributing 90% of Columbian Cocaine on city streets at the height of Washington, DC crack epidemic in 1987"(Go to website: http://www.imdb.com/title/ tt1220567/ plotsummary? Order movie "Life of Rayful Edmonds III).* It was the beginning of birth pains in our major cities. I clearly remember those days; it broke my heart to see our young African American males die on the streets from Washington, DC to Los Angeles, CA, all behind greed. Think about how I felt, I was not much older than these guys that was dying myself, I was blessed enough to be in the military and working at the time. Not very long after that; the 1990s kicked in and things got worse. The Rap music that I grew up on as a teenager that hit in the summer of 1979 was fun, exciting and had a positive message. Some-how it changed to promoting guns, gangs and violence and our children minds were consumed by it. Very few people saw where this was going, but I knew it, I saw what was getting ready to happen to our young people and because of it, I got angry, became very serious about my personal walk with God and took a stand against BET and MTV. It was all coming from the television music videos. I realized that music videos on television had a lot of influence on the minds of young people and would get a lot of them killed. If you asked me back then, but I thought BET and MTV had done more to assist in thekilling of young people than the Vietnam War. I was that upset during those days.

I remember on Christmas day before I left Washington DC in 1989 to move back to Denver, Colorado. I was invited over some Christian friends' home with several others. We were all watching television when a Hip Hop music video came on the large set. The video was clearly projecting young black men going after money, cars, sex, violence and drugs. Right there in my friend's living room the spirit of God rose up in me for the first time. I was very upset as to what I was seeing and many said to me later that I went off that night. I didn't realize it at the time, but preached my first message in that living room on the destructive lyrics in hip-hop music (in which I loved Hip-Hop, I am first generation Hip-Hop) and how it was killing our young people. I knew that I had to do something. God had spoken to me a few months before that Christmas and said *"I want you to help my young people."* It became clear to me a few months later what he wanted me to do. When I arrived to Denver in January 1990, I was all business. I got back in the Word of God and it wasn't long before I started a men's breakfast ministry one Sunday per month in our church. A few months later I was asked to be my Pastor's *"Aide."* The next year I was preaching as a young minister and assisting the Pastor with men and counseling. The rest is history as I began conducting concert outreaches with Christian hip hop artist to get the gospel out to the young people. It was music that I knew that I couldn't deny and was going to be around for the long hall. Here we are now in the Twenty-First Century and we have an entire generation of young people who have made chasing after the money epidemic through Hip-Hop music that focuses on greed. Not all Hip-Hop music is this way, but there is enough out there that have influenced the minds of many to destruction. It's to the point that very few in this generation want to seek after an education, trade or skill. Once again, I grew up on Hip Hop music when it first came out, it did not used to be that way. It's all about the money now; education, trade and skill has taken a back seat to songs and movies that say to the young people *"Get Rich or Die Tryin,"* released on February 6, 2003. Do you not think that our young people take lyrics like that serious? What I have seen in our young people makes me think of a story in the bible that I have read many times about Shadrach, Meshach, and Abendego. I am aware that many of you may have read it, but probably never seen it like God has showed it to me as to what is happening with the young generation in America. If you remember, King Nebuchadnezzar made an image of gold 90 feet high and nine feet wide and set it in the plain of Dura. I believe this image of gold that he set up was an image of *"himself."* The bible doesn't give any details about the image. The interesting thing is that he wanted all the people, no matter their nationality or belief, if they were living in the Provinces of Babylon, to bow down at a certain time and worship this large golden image.

Just like our day, gold in King Nebuchadnezzar's day represented money, power, influence and wealth. He makes a decree that everyone is to do this and he sends out his officials to see to it that everybody in his province understands this and knows to do it or it will cause them their very life. I find it very strange that in order to get the people to know when to bow down and worship this golden image that represents (money, power, influence and wealth the King possessed) he uses his representatives and music to get it done. The people were told by a herald: *"This is what you are commanded to do,*

O peoples, nations and men of every language: As soon as you hear the sound of the horn, flute, zither, lyre, harp, pipes and all kinds of music, you must fall down and worship the image of gold that King Nebuchadnezzar has set up. Whoever does not fall down and worship will immediately be thrown into a blazing furnace" (Daniel 3:4). If you read the entire story you will see that Shadrach, Meshach, and Abendego refused to do it and was thrown into the fire, but miraculously delivered out by God's mighty hand.

Why do I depict this story and *"what does it has to do with the price of tea in China or Greed in the lyrics of Music?"* The Word of God teaches us *"What has been will be again, what has been done will be done again; there is nothing new under the sun"* (*Ecclesiastes 1:9*). If the devil had men and women bowing down to the image that represented money, wealth and power and music back in Daniels day, what makes you think that it can't happen again in our day? We are seeing it right before our eyes. World champion boxers and wrestlers can't take the ring without excessive items draped around them and music that promotes wealth, power and greed playing in the background. They want the crowd to bow down to them and worship them. The people in Daniel's day where in a trance when they heard the music as they bowed down and worshipped the 90 foot golden image of money, wealth, power and greed. That same spirit is in the earth attacking our young generation and putting them in that same trance. They have no understanding of the power of bad music and lyrics. I say *"People act out what they think about."* If I am putting bad thoughts in your mind through music and videos then you will eventually start acting them out. Do you realize that many have died on the streets behind a song(s) that they continued to play over and over again and allowed in their spirit? All music is designed to get in your thoughts in order to sell, but when it gets down in your soul, that can be dangerous. Music can be addictive, hepatizing, memorizing and destructive. Many of these artists want your children to buy their music, bow down and worship them. The pride, arrogance and ignorance that's in them is heart wrenching. Why can't they make songs that motivates, stimulates or edifies our young people's conscious? The reason is that they don't think it will sell. As a parent, my own children were born in this generation I am speaking about and I saw how this music impacted their thoughts and their lives. It swept through society like a storm and caused more problems than you can imagine. I constantly warned my children about the power of music and its lyrics. Both of my sons are talented music writers and artist. I admit that it caused a strong rift between us in the past, but now that they are older and of age, they understand the power of music and what I was saying to them when they were younger to protect them as their dad. They have seen for themselves in the music industry and from the stage how music can influence the minds of people. They know what it is like to see someone get shot because someone took the lyrics of another person's song too far.

Subsequently, I can think of a day I was home in down town Rochester, New York and I saw these boys doing the most bazaar dance I have ever seen. They were dancing very wildly and I noticed that after a few seconds, each of them one by one would throw themselves down to the ground flat on their backs and bounce back up. I thought; this is weird, what kind of dance is that? It looked like it hurt. They would just fall to the ground. Again, I thought to myself, now that is odd. But I noticed that they just kept doing it. This being where I grew up, I knew that kids in Rochester don't do things unless it is something new. A few weeks later, I noticed another young man (who was in this same age group as the boys I saw dancing downtown) watching this weird kind of dancing video on a computer. I thought it looked familiar and asked him *"what kind of dancing is that, for I saw some kids a few weeks ago doing it downtown"*? He gladly said *"it's called 5000 – which means 'Go Stupid'"*. When I watched it more closely, I saw many kids falling down to the floor to the beat of the music. I said to myself, *"Oh my God,"* immediately I was reminded once again of the story of King Nebuchadnezzar and the three Hebrew boys (Shadrach, Meshach, and Abendego who would not fall down and worship the 90 foot golden image).

I noticed that the kids were dancing to this aggressive Hip Hop music and it was at that moment the Lord gave me the revelation as to what was happening in the spirit realm in the world with our youth. The devil have not only have hypnotized these kids to love this music, but they now fall down in worship to it through a dance called *"5000"*. I know you may think that this might be a stretch, but I have to tell it like it is. It was happening again in our day.

Here is a fact for you to check out that I have done some research on. History itself shows that one of the vilest leaders - Adolf Hitler knew how to use the power of music, dance and lyrics to get his young generation to be loyal and committed to his philosophy or military agenda. Hitler established a young Semi-professional band called the Sturm-Abteilung undHitlerjugend. *"The Sturm-Abteilung was no more than a political and ideological organization made up of kids. Their emphasis was put upon military and fighting songs, through which the **10 to 18 year olds** could reaffirm their commitment to Adolf Hitler and his ideology. This was to result in the youngsters, (whose **lusty singing and marching** was a complete* *world away from traditional German military music),* **taking a rebellious pride** *in the fact that all their early activities were performed without any help from the experts, rejecting the 'know-it-all' attitudes of their musical peers! Gradually the Hitlerjugend evolved into a* **powerful political youth organization** *whose leadership began to control every aspect of music and gifted youngsters were sent to the* Musikschulen für Jugend und Volk *and from this early 'rag-tag' musical education of Sturm-Abteilung* **street-fighting songs** *would come many talented future* Wehrmacht *and* Waffen-SS *military bandsmen, conductors and musical directors (See http:// www.tomahawkfilms.com/jugend.htm)."*

There are six things here that I don't want you to miss. Hitler established this musical group so that they could be loyal to his ideas. He targeted the 10 to 18 year old children. This is when kids are most impressionable and are not thinking at their best. The kids in the band weren't singing modern day German music, but music of their own with a militant and fighting spirit. Hmmm, does that sound familiar? Hitler was no fool; he was not only demonic, but very smart. He got to his nations youth's mind through music. They were singing lusty lyrics and marching (dancing) sexually. Boy, doesn't that sound like what is going on with our young people music videos today. They were taking rebellious pride in their songs, music, and marching as if their peer artist didn't know a thing about music and they knew more. Shall I stop here? Their music had a political agenda and they were no more than street fighting songs. I think I'll stop. The rest you can think about on your own.

I often wonder what some of American greats like Dr. Martin Luther King, Malcolm X, John F. Kennedy and Bobby

Kennedy would think about this generation if they were living today. What would they think of their hard service and work to make this nation a better place for all men to live? Would they think these were the civil rights that they fought for to see our young people murdering each other in the streets behind money, sex, drugs and music? I often wonder what their speeches would sound like today. To be honest with you, I think many of them would pass out from a broken heart. They would have never needed an assassin's bullet. The disappointment of young America today would have given them a heart attack. Some way America has to take back its moral fiber through its music. I'm compelling Rap artist all over who read this book to watch your lyrics. It's nothing wrong with Rap; it's how you are using it to control the minds of an entire generation for evil, which is wrong. Stop bowing to the devil and worshipping the gold and silver it has to offer. God can use your gift to encourage, rejoice, inspire, motivate and uplift. That doesn't mean you have to do gospel music, but you can do something better than what has been done for money and massive destruction.

I will end this chapter with this one last surprising story. At the time of completing this book and cleaning up this chapter, I just so happened to be at work and spoke with a man over the phone who at the time I thought was from India. As I continued the conversation with him I came to know that he was a small business owner and had four businesses in the state of California. He was a very positive and pleasant man. His last name was Naji, therefore I thought of one of my favorite R&B Jazz Artist *"Najee."* I asked him if he liked jazz music. I told him that there was a jazz artist that had his same name, but spelled it differently. He went on to tell me that he did not listen to music very much and he did not like a lot of the music of today. That got my attention since I was working on this chapter *"Greed in the Lyrics of Music."* I went on to ask him why and what kind of music did he listen to from time to time when he did listen to it. He would go on to tell me, *"Country and Hip – Hop from the 1970s and 1980s."* I found that very interesting, still thinking he was from India. I asked why Hip-Hop from that error? He would go on to tell me that the Hip-Hop from that error was more positive and had a message in it. He would begin to talk unfavorably about the Hip-Hop from the 1990s and on. I could not believe that I was on the phone with a man that I thought who was from India about the very things I was writing in my latest book. He began to talk about how it has influenced gangs, sex, drugs and violence and he did not want to have anything to do with it. He explained how it didn't produce anything good in the young people. As we continued to talk I told him that I was an author and was writing a book and what he was saying to me I talk a lot about in one of the chapters concerning the spirit of Greed in the lyrics of music, particularly Hip-Hop from the 1990s and on. He was surprised. At this point he really opened up to me and started talking about his faith and how he was raised by his dad. He told me that he has been living in America for the past 14 years and how good this country has been to him and excepting of all people, but has changed. He explained how concerned he was about the gangs, drugs and violence in the country. I certainly felt that this was a God ordained phone call and so did he. I was very intrigued that I could be talking to a foreigner and he would have the same concerns that I would have with young people in our nation. He was a God fearing man and I rightly assumed he was of the Muslim faith. When I finally asked him where he was from he said he was *"Arabic."* I told him that I thought he was from India. I asked him exactly where he was from and the man told me that he was from *"Yemen."* Not only was I wrong about where he was from, but also I would learn he was only 25 years old. I thought I had been speaking to someone much, much older. That means he had been in this country since he was 11 years old and he told me that he had been following the teachings of his father and has become a successful business man in this country. Here I was talking to a man who is from one of the very countries that has been recently banned from coming to America to seek refuge, but has become a successful productive citizen and can see the some of the mistakes our young people are making in following the lyrics of greed in their music.

Chapter Nine

Greed in Business and Corporate America

"Then he said to them, "Watch out! Be on your guard against all kinds of greed; a man's life does not consist in the abundance of his possessions." (Luke 12:15)

I'm sure that some of you were thinking "when is he going to talk about the greed that transpires in business and corporate America?" I have been waiting to talk about this subject for I believe it is one the main subjects that God wanted me to write about and may have delayed the writing of this book. I started this book in early 2007 and since then, I have done some business and contracting for myself in the insurance industry. The things that I have seen with greed in business and corporate America are staggering. Let me qualify this chapter by first saying this. Once you walk with God for a-while you start learning how God communicates to you things that he wants you learn about and help others with later. I can't speak for anyone else, but for me, He allows me to either see things or experience them to gain spiritual insight on the subject. What I am going to write about in this chapter I have either seen, experienced or have gained knowledge through watching.

Business is a very sensitive subject for most Christians. Many Christians don't think that God's people should be involved in secular business, but only be involved in business that edifies God. There are others that believe that if you are involved in secular business you should be in business with other Christians. Before we can talk about the spirit of greed in business, let me start off by saying…business is exactly what it is…business. Whether it's a Christian business or non-Christian, it's about creating jobs and generating revenue. It's about getting a return on your investment.

The Spirit of Greed shows up in business whether it is a Christian or Secular, if there is such a thing. I worked in the insurance industry that put me in front of a lot of what we would call the *"decision makers."* This would be the CEO, President, COO, Human Resources Director, Office Managers…etc. I talk to a lot of employers and employees. When you spend a considerable amount of time talking to employers, you get a well-rounded idea of how employers think and treat their employees.

First of all, I would like to say hats off to all those employers who I have meet in the past years and they truly care about their employees. I have meet some of the greatest leaders that have their employees best interest in mind and their employees have no idea how blessed they are to work for such a person or company. Whether it is temporary employment or long-term, there are still many employers out there that do things in a spirit that is not greed and it pleases God. Likewise, I will tell you that each and every one of these people I have meet, their business are doing well even in difficult economic times above their competitors.

Unfortunately, on the opposite end, I have to admit that I have regularly meet employers who do not think and feel this way about their employees. Their attitudes about their workers were mind-boggling. At times I could not believe what I was hearing from some of these employers as I went over different benefit plans. Many times it was discouraging and depressing, but it was not my business to change employers mind in how they felt about their workers, but to offer them benefit solutions that would have interest in. What do you think the situation was for most of these companies that had this kind of attitude? You guessed it! I noticed that many of these businesses struggled in the market place and were on a verge of closing. If only they could see the attitudes of their competitors that did well in a down-turned economy verses their thinking towards the workers. What they could not see is that their lack of success had a lot to do with their attitude and how they treated their employees. They were too focused on a return on investment for themselves. What they couldn't see how the guy or gal across town (that provided the same business) prospered. You talk about attitude determining your altitude; I have seen it in business in both Christian and Non-Christian companies. This tells me that the idea of having a Christian business has nothing to do with success. It has everything to do with your outlook on the welfare of the people that God gives you to be responsible for. I know plenty of Christian businesses that have failed because of their sub-par attitude towards their employees. They too close everyday just like any other company. I can stay on this subject all day with writing, but you get the picture. What I am saying to you is that no one told me this neither did I read it in a book. I saw this attitude several times on a weekly basis. Once again, my job was not to try to convert the employer to change his/her views about how they treated their workers and run their business. But, sometimes I just wanted to say, *"Hey; there are principals on how you as an employer can treat your people and God will honor your efforts."* It doesn't matter whether your business is Christian on Non-Christian, the principles of giving, concern and respect for others will work in any organization. I have walked into some of these successful companies and immediately you can feel in the peacefulness in the atmosphere. The attitude of the receptionist at the front desk is second to none. Mind you, this spirit is not in every business. When I talk with these decision makers, they are the kind of people that you want to join them at their next company picnic. Their attitudes are very pleasant. I noticed that their employees enjoyed working there and they realized that they have perks and benefits that many in the work force are not getting. I say again, these are not always Christian business owners. They are business owners who understand how to treat their employees in order to succeed in the market place. Simple respect for others!

The temptation to do business unfairly is all too prevalent in our world today. It doesn't matter if it is a corporate giant or a small mom & pop local store. Too many owners are not treating their employee's decently and they wonder why they struggle and their talented folks continue to leave. These companies make their employees do hard work for very little pay. Many of these companies will not promote certain races or sex into different positions and will fire them at the drop of a hat. They use fear tactics and lack of appreciation to control their workers. That is not success, that's called *"Tyranny."*

First of all, let's address this low pay issue across the nation. I have meet so many people who are upset because their employer pays them so little that they can't afford certain basic needs. When I hear how much some people are getting paid I'm almost offended myself. I have meet employers who are interested in doing business for themselves, but have no interest in seeing to it that their employees benefit as well. Any employer who thinks that their people can live off $8.00 per hour in today's economy is out of touch with reality. I have had employers flat out tell me in our meetings to *"take care of me, it's about me and my family being taken of, I'm not thinking about my employees."* I mean this has been a real wake up call for me. The business owners who have these attitudes don't realize the only reason why they have the employees that they have is because they don't feel like they can go anywhere else at the time. I hate to say it, but it must be said, we have business owners out here that don't deserve anyone working for them. Business is a two-way street! If they want to treat people like that, they need to keep the hiring to relatives and treat their own family members like that not other people, slavery was abolished in this country over 150 years ago.

The point is that, how you treat your employees will determine God's hand in your business. He appreciates you being an employer and giving people jobs, but to only be in the business for yourself is no less than a Spirit of Greed. Why do you think America's economy has been so bad for the past years? Could it be the unfairness in the market place and selfish employers? Did you know when it comes to the subject of economic inequality in America that *"the top 20% of income earners (Corporate America) in the United States own nearly 84 percent of the wealth and the bottom 40% combine for a meager 0.3%? The Walton family, for example, has more wealth than 42% of American families combined."* *(*Article:

Scientific American - Economic Inequality in America, Its Far Worse than you think; dated March 31, 2015 by Nicholas Fitz). Comedian/Actor – Chris Rock said in the fall of 2014 to New York Times columnist Frank Rich, *"Oh people don't even know. If poor people knew how rich rich people are, there would be riots in the streets."*

Consequently, I have seen companies flourish who treat their employees well and the employees weren't smart enough to realize how blessed they were to work for someone like they did. It's all a matter of perception. Some people can't see when they are being treated well and others can. The prophet Jeremiah said, this is what the LORD says: *"Cursed is the one who trusts in man, who depends on flesh for his strength and whose heart turns away from the LORD. He will be like a bush in the wastelands; they will not see prosperity when it comes" Jeremiah 17:5-6*. Many employees don't know when they have a good thing. The one thing that is clear, these companies that I have experienced are doing quite well. I'm certain the way they pay and treat their employees have a lot to do with their great quarterly results. Unfortunately, greed is everywhere, including in business. The temptations for the ones that have to take advantage of the ones that have not are ever prevalent in the workplace. I know that these employers do not have the employee best interest at hand. Regardless to this fact, people have to work and pay the bills. Nevertheless, they put up with a bad situation as long as they can. I learned long time ago that I am definitely not one for unfairness. I have had good employers and bad ones. Some-times you have a good employer, but a crazy supervisor. The point is that you must take these experiences and know that companies that treat their people right - prosper. If you are in a company that does not treat their people right, you may want to have your resume out on-line some-where.

Companies that are not in it for them-self share the wealth with their people. They have raises, incentive programs, benefits, paid time off…etc. I can tell you that there are some businesses in society that are not trying to give their employers no more than a few dollars a week in order to keep them working and that is it! These employees can forget about their employers thinking about any kind of incentive programs to share the wealth even when the business prospers. You can take this like you want it, but no one should not have to put up with something like this for very long. Work for them and do your job well, don't be a slacker, but pray and seek new employment and when you can make your break don't look back. God will free you from this kind of oppression.

Finally, be on guard against all kinds of greed, not just in business. There is a story in the bible where Jesus took on the subject of greed in a business transaction between two brothers. It was an inheritance that needed to be divided up properly and the brother who felt he was being cheated out of his portion confronted the Lord to help him...."*Someone in the crowd said to him, "Teacher, tell my brother to divide the inheritance with me." Jesus replied, "Man, who appointed me a judge or an arbiter between you?" Then he said to them, "Watch out! Be on your guard against all kinds of greed; a man's life does not consist in the abundance of his possessions"(Luke 12:13-15).*

Notice that Jesus didn't address the other brother to do right by his brother. In fact, Jesus warned the upset brother to guard himself against all kinds of greed. I hope you got that. He said *"all kinds of greed"*. There are different kinds of greed. That's why I'm writing this book *"The Spirit of Greed."* Christ knew that greed didn't only manifest through monetary gain, but in many different ways. Greed comes from a very selfish spirit. It only has itself in mind. This brother was clearly only thinking about himself if he didn't want to divide up the inheritance with his sibling properly. On the contrary, Jesus was warning the offended brother against the same spirit over taking him that was clearly in his selfish brother. Jesus lets us know that LIFE does not consist in the abundance of a man's possessions.

How many times in your life have you been promoted to have a lot of possessions? There is nothing wrong with having possessions the real problem is when a person thinks that their life consist of it. Nothing we have or ever attain can leave this world with us, so why do we sell our soul to maintain so little? I enjoy work. I like working hard. I believe in hard work. Also, I believe in enjoying what comes to my pocket as a result of my work. But, I don't ever want to get caught up in thinking that my life consist in things that I have. I know life is not in stuff. Stuff comes and goes. Life is in what we do to advance the Kingdom of God on earth, but you can't do that broke! Once our name is called to heaven, life ceases here in this world and new life starts above! Solomon said it this way, *"Enjoy life with your wife, whom you love, all the days of this meaningless life that God has given you under the sun— all your meaningless days. For this is your lot in life and in your toilsome labor under the sun. Whatever your hand finds to do, do it with all your might, for in the grave, where you are going, there is neither working nor planning nor knowledge nor wisdom"* (*Ecclesiastes 9:9-1*).

There is no need for you to ever be greedy in business. God gives us business ideas to be faithful over for His glory. If your business can employ people, than good for you, treat them right and share the increase wisely. None of it can go with you to the grave anyway. If you treat people right and it pleases God, there will be enough for you, your employees, and to leave for your children and children's children. *"Stay Kingdom!"* Don't be bound by a Spirit of Greed in business.

Chapter Ten

Watch out for Greed in your Neighbors

"You shall not covet your neighbor's house. You shall not covet your neighbor's wife, or his manservant or maidservant, his ox or donkey, or anything that belongs to your neighbor." (Exodus 20:17)

Now I can get to the chapter where most of us live, dealing with the spirit of Greed in your neighbor. When I was a kid I remember when someone got a new bike, car, furniture, television, clothes, you name it. It seemed to spread in the neighborhood like wildfire. To be honest with you, I remember my mother doing things like moving in our new furniture, stereo, or television in at night so people wouldn't know what she just purchased. We were told that we could not have a lot of kids in the house - only certain kids that she knew could come inside and play. I didn't fully understand what she was doing until one day we came home and someone had broken into our house. They stole a brand new television and squirted lotion all over my mother's new bedroom set. Our home would get broken into about two or three times.

I remember each time feeling like we had just been raped. It was a strange feeling to come home and things were missing that you enjoyed for so long. When this happened I was about 10 years old and attending a Catholic school where the Nuns taught you the Ten Commandments. I really wasn't a bible student, but I respected all of the Commandments and what the Nuns taught. When this happened all I could think of is the commandment that said *"Thou shall not steal" (Exodus 20:15)*. At that time, where I lived, there were a whole lot of people disregarding that verse. Stealing was a way of life for many and my mother knew it. When people are stolen from they experience an onslaught of emotions. They become angry, sad, hurt, distant…etc. Many times a person can blame others or themselves for what was stolen. Whatever the feelings, there is a reason why God said *"Thou shall not steal."* First of all, I am not here to talk about theft, but I am here to talk about something that has to do with theft that goes on in each of our world. We must understand when somebody steals something that you have - it is because they like what you own. I never realized how much people secretly desire other peoples stuff and will scheme to get it. It is an ugly spirit that has lurked in our homes, churches, businesses, and communities since the existence of man. There are people who live their whole lives stealing what others have and never really work to get their own. They con-artist that have figured out that it is easier to live off what others may have rather work for themselves. You may ask yourself, *"How are they able to do such things?"* I say, they have learned the *"gift of gab"* and can talk their way in and out of any situation. They are *"covetous."* It means; *"having or showing a great desire to possess something, typically something belonging to someone else."* God knew about these folk as far back as the days of Moses. He knew that there would be people in the earth who would rather covet your house, wife, money, possessions, gifts, talents and not be willing to work for their own success. He knew that, to them, it is easier to take somebody else's possessions. Therefore, he had to warn the people that *"You shall not covet your neighbor's house. You shall not covet your neighbor's wife, or his manservant or maidservant, his ox or donkey, or anything that belongs to your neighbor" (Exodus 20:17).*

Notice in the verse that everything belonged to the neighbor. Do you have any idea how much covetousness that is around you each day? Do you understand how many times someone covets the littlest things that you may have, even if it is just a good relationship with a friend? People are greedy for all kinds of gain. It's sad, but true! Greed is in people everywhere. Unfortunately, so many of us listen to people who talk us out of our good situation only to find out is that those people want what we got. Years ago, I was talking to a friend about how I met a Pastor (who is well known) and established a good relationship with him. After doing so, I realized that several people in my life became jealous and would question how did we meet and make sly remarks towards it. I would for the most part just ignore them or say it was a *"divine connection"* and God did it for his purpose in the earth. Nevertheless, I have grown spiritually leaps and bounds because my connection to him. I saw that even in the slightest relationships that you have people who covetousness and jealous of what you have. If we all look closely in and around our lives, there is a good chance of someone coveting your spouse, car, home, life-style, gifts, talents, relationships… you name it. Covetousness is an unclean spirit that is bound up in greed. Life should not be this way, but unfortunately, this spirit is in so many in the world. It puts you in a real position that you have to be careful as to who you tell your earnest dreams and aspirations. If it was not true, take a look what happened to the young Joseph when he told his brothers his dreams:

Now Israel loved Joseph more than any of his other sons, because he had been born to him in his old age; and he made a richly ornamented robe for him. When his brothers saw that their father loved him more than any of them they hated him and could not speak a kind word to him. Joseph had a dream, and when he told it to his brothers, they hated him all the more. He said to them, "Listen to this dream I had: We were binding sheaves of grain out in the field when suddenly my sheaf rose and stood upright, while your sheaves gathered around mine and bowed down to it." His brothers said to him, "Do you intend to reign over us? Will you actually rule us?"

And they hated him all the more because of his dream and what he had said. Then he had another dream, and he told it to his brothers. "Listen," he said, "I had another dream, and this time the sun and moon and eleven stars were bowing down to me."

When he told his father as well as his brothers, his father rebuked him and said, "What is this dream you had? Will your mother and I and your brothers actually come and bow down to the ground before you?" His brothers were jealous of him, but his father kept the matter in mind.

Now his brothers had gone to graze their father's flocks near Shechem, and Israel said to Joseph, "As you know, your brother's are grazing the flocks near Shechem. Come, I am going to send you to them." "Very well," he replied. So he said to him, "Go and see if all is well with your brothers and with the flocks, and bring word back to me." Then he sent him off from the Valley of Hebron. When Joseph arrived at Shechem, a man found him wandering around in the fields and asked him,

"What are you looking for?" He replied, "I'm looking for my brothers. Can you tell me where they are grazing their flocks?"

"They have moved on from here," the man answered. "I heard them say, 'Let's go to Dothan.'" So Joseph went after his brothers and found them near Dothan. But they saw him in the distance, and before he reached them, they plotted to kill him.

"Here comes that dreamer!" they said to each other. "Come now, let's kill him and throw him into one of these cisterns and say that a ferocious animal devoured him. Then we'll see what comes of his dreams...etc" (Genesis 37:3-20).

They planned and plotted to kill their own brother. Why did they do this, because they were jealous of him and covetous of the relationship that he had with their father. The dreams that Joseph had made them fear that he would one day rule over them. But in essence, God had plans for him to rise to power, save his family and the entire nation from an up and coming famine. God had the preservation of Israel already in mind when Joseph was only 17 years old and showed him the dreams that he had. Therefore, his brothers were not only upset with the relationship that he had with their father, but the fact that God was speaking to their younger brother through dreams and made plans to throw him in the pit and get rid of him. I have a saying that I like to warn people who become haters, *"be careful who you choose to throw in the pit; for it can be that very person that God is planning to use to bring you out of your up and coming famine."* My mother understood jealousy and covetousness when I was a kid. Covetousness is a spirit that is wrapped up in jealously. It means that somebody wants what you have instead of possessing their own. It's a dangerous spirit that just won't quit in this world. The next time you think things are safe in your care, watch out! Covetousness can be lurking in your neighbor that you care so much about. Greed, jealousy or covetousness are all *"kissing cousins"* and in the same family for destruction. Be mindful of what goes in your spirit and ask the Lord in prayer to deliver you from the spirit of Greed and covetousness.

Chapter Eleven
Greed, Jealousy and Government

"You were blameless in your ways from the day you were created till wickedness was found in you, through your Wide-spread trade you were filled with violence, and you sinned". Ezekiel 28:15-16

Therefore rejoice you heavens and you who dwell in them! But woe to the earth and the sea, because the devil has gone down to you! He is filled with fury, because he knows that his time is short." Revelations 12:12

Interesting enough it looks like I will conclude this book with how I started it. If we are going to fully understand the spirit of Greed we are going to have to look a lot closer at jealously. I know that I eluded to this a little in the previous chapter as we can see it grow out of covetousness, but what I want to do is take a closer look as to what was in the devil from the beginning and how it is impacting our world today. When I started this book in early 2007, after writing "CHOOSE," I went on a business assignment to Phoenix, Arizona from October to November 2007. I thought to myself "great, I can finish up my first draft of *'The Spirit of Greed'* while in my hotel room during the evenings and weekends." For days I could not continue to write this book, nothing was coming. There was complete silence from the Lord, until one day I was in my hotel room staring at my computer and I heard the Holy Spirit say to me *"put this aside for now, there are more things I need to show you before you can fully understand this subject."* I was amazed, but I knew what I had just heard. There was no one else in the room but me. By faith I put my laptop away and concentrated only on my business assignment in Arizona, it would be a very busy time.

Two months later, the Spirit of the Lord would give me another book to start writing, which became my second book *"Choose II, How to Overcome the Betrayals we Experience in Life."* This book came strong and fast and I had my first draft done in a matter of a few months. I concentrated all my efforts in 2008 on writing this book only to start another book *"Everybody Needs a Coach"* in 2009. Unfortunately no word from heaven on *"the Spirit of Greed."* I knew I needed to finish this project but was faithfully waiting on the Lord when to pick it back up. I would not get the go ahead until early 2015. By this time it had been another eight years and boy was there a lot that the Lord made me see during this eight year period for me to really understand this spirit called *"greed."* I will get to all that later, it was a lot and we are going to talk about it.

Firstly, let's go back to what was found in the devil in heaven. We know that he was a great Cherub at one time until iniquity was found in him; *"you were blameless in your ways from the day you were created till wickedness was found in you"* (Ezekiel 28:15). The question is *"what was found in the devil?"* We know from the earlier chapter that it was "greed" that was found in him. But I want to look into a few other things in the bible that will give us an even clearer picture of all that was in the devil. Why would I do this? Well, while the heavens and all its inhabitants were told to rejoice (because the devil had been thrown out from them). We were warned in Revelations 12:12 *"Woe to the inhabitants of the earth and of the sea! For the devil is come down into you."* I think that is worth investigating and why? Let us ask ourselves *"what did the devil bring down to the earth that is no longer in the heavens that the inhabitants are rejoicing over?"* Nevertheless, whatever it is, we have to deal with it here on earth.

I have done my research and found it to be *"jealously,"* not just jealously, but *"jealously over the wisdom of God"* was found in him. Let's take a look at the first trouble the devil caused when he and one-third of the angels were thrown down to the earth. First may I add, that was not a promotion for them, this was a demotion. Anytime you have from heaven to earth (unless you are Jesus) you have just gone backwards. In Genesis 3:1-5; the devil has a conversation with Eve that causes the fall of man in the Garden of Eden. The bible say's in the verses above; *"Now the serpent was craftier than any of the wild animals the Lord God had made. He said to the woman, "Did God really say, 'You must not eat from any tree in the garden?" The woman said to the serpent, "We may eat fruit from the trees in the garden, but God did say, 'You must not eat fruit from the tree that is in the middle of the garden, and you must not touch it or you will die.'" "You will not surely die," the serpent said to the woman. For God knows that when you eat of it your eyes will be opened and you will be like God, knowing good and evil."* The knowledge of good and evil was the very wisdom of God and the devil knew it; therefore He used his craftiness to cause the woman and the man to fall in the garden with tempting them that they will be like God or wise as "gods." The iniquity that was found in the devil was his jealously over God's wisdom. Although the devil was created as wise, He was not as wise as God. This was the jealousy that came down to the earth that tried to disrupt heaven and all its inhabitants.

A chapter later in Genesis 4:1-8, we see the first murder in the earth and it came from jealously that was in one brother over the other. It say's *"Adam lay with his wife Eve, and she became pregnant and gave birth to Cain. She said, "With the help of the Lord I have brought forth a man." Later she gave birth to his brother Abel. Now Abel kept flocks and Cain worked the soil. I the course of time Cain brought some of the fruits of the soil as an offering to the Lord. But Abel brought fat portions from some of the firstborn of his flock. The Lord looked with favor on Abel and his offering, but on Cain and his offering He did not look with favor. So Cain was very angry and his face was downcast. Then the Lord said to Cain, "Why is your face downcast? If you do what is right, will you not be accepted? But if you do not do what is right, sin is crouching at your door; it desires to have you, but you must master it."* Can I tell you that the sin that was crouching at his door was *"jealousy,"* and he did not master. It goes on to say, *"Now Cain said to his brother Abel, "Let's go out to the field"* (He should have said *"for what?") And while they were in the field, Cain attacked his brother Abel and killed him.* Here in the bible is the account of the first murder in the earth all behind jealously, not only jealously, but Cain was jealous of his brother's wisdom in knowing what was right in pleasing God to have his offering accepted with favor.

Let's go a little bit deeper. How about the jealousy Rebekah had in her heart over the birth right and favor that her husband Isaac had for their older son Esau verses his younger brother Jacob? Tell me this wasn't a *"hot mess"* and jealousy at its best work. This would have been a good "Reality TV show" in today's world. The length of planning and scheming she would go through just to see to it that the birth right and pronounced blessing from her husband Isaac would go to the younger instead of the intended older son. Do I even need to write the story? You can read it on your own in Genesis 27:143. It is a classic story of lies, jealousy, scheming and betrayal in one household that has had catastrophic national and historical issues behind it until this day. The point I am trying to make is that jealousy has been around since the heavens and it came down to the earth through the devil and has gotten into mankind. Can I prove it? Shall I go deeper? Lord have mercy! Now I know why the Lord wanted me to put this project aside for a time until I have learned and seen more. Remember I said earlier in this chapter that the Lord has allowed me to see a lot over the past eight years and that we would talk about it? We'll, here it comes. I am going to share with you what God wanted me to see that had not happened yet at the time I started this book that is wrapped up in the Spirit of Greed.

In 2007; several events had not happened neither did I for see them coming as I end this project at the end of December 2016. You've all guessed it, the jealously and greed for power in over our nation. We have witnessed as Americans the most ugly, divisive, bitter, angry, fault finding presidential campaigns and elections in modern history. Do you remember the verse I used to open chapter five (The Spirit of Greed in Relationships) *"Who is wise and understanding among you? Let him show it by his good life by deeds done in the humility that comes from wisdom. But if you harbor bitter envy and selfish ambition in your hearts, do not boast about it or deny the truth. Such 'wisdom' does not come down from heaven, but is earthly, unspiritual, of the devil. For where you have envy and selfish ambition, there you find disorder and every evil practice; James 3:13-16 (NIV)?"* What started it all and? Let's focus on the second, third and fourth part of this verse; *But if you harbor bitter envy and selfish ambition in your hearts, do not boast about it or deny the truth. Such 'wisdom' does not come down from heaven, but is earthly, unspiritual, of the devil. For where you have envy and selfish ambition, there you find disorder and every evil practice; James 3:13-16 (NIV)."*

On November 4th, 2008; America voted in office its 44th President, Barrack Hussein Obama. This was the first time in American history that we had a president that was African American. All 43 of his presidential predecessors where white males. Special Note: *I highly advise if you are looking for a place to stop reading, right here would be a great place to close the book and jump ship. But if you are really interested in learning more about the spirit of Greed, its behaviors and attitudes regardless of what race or sex it's in, then keep reading.* America could have never forecasted a black man coming to power to run the highest office in the world. It shocked everyone in this nation. People were in the streets on that election night celebrating, crying and reminiscing all those who fought so hard for civil rights in the 1960s and those who suffered on the slave ships to America that either died in route or were mistreated heavily not as men, but as property in this country for 245 years.

It was a solid slap in the face to many, but not all caucasians who were taught in their lives that a black man cannot lead and he/she by nature of the color of their skin is inferior to white people. Let me give a little history about race in America since my birth. I was born in August 1963. I was barely three months old; while my mother (20 years old at the time) was sitting on the couch, watching television, feeding me a bottle when her program was interrupted with "Breaking News;" the Former President John F. Kennedy had just been shot and killed by an assassin in Dallas, TX., stemming from all the racial tension and bigotry in America at the time. Not only was he Catholic and feared to be a puppet President for the Pope, but he was a supporter of civil rights and called an *"n*gger lover"* by many whites. I was a year and half old when the Advocate for a separate nation for blacks in America "Malcolm X" was killed by a Nation of Islam member while speaking at a rally for his organization in New York City. I was four years old when the leader of the civil rights movement, Dr. Martin Luther King Jr., was shot and killed by an assassin's bullet while standing on the balcony outside of his second-story motel room in Memphis, TN. Lastly, I was still four years old when Former Senator Robert Kennedy (President John F. Kennedy's brother) was shot and killed by Sirhan Sirhan during a presidential primaries appearance because he objected to Robert Kennedy's support for Israel in the 1967 *"Six-Day War."* All of these assassinations and deaths to leaders in this nation happened before I turned five years old and entered the kindergarten. It was the basis from which I am coming to say something about what has been going wrong in this country for the past 50 years. This was the world I was born in and have looked for answers to understand why? I have to say that I it was my earnest desire that this division amongst us would be over with by the time I reached adulthood so that my children and grandchildren would not have to deal with any of this foolishness. After watching the attitudes of many Americans during the 2016 Presidential Campaign, it opened my eyes to how much progress that we have not made concerning race relations in this country since the 1960s. Race has always been a problem in America, there is no hiding it. Power and jealously over who controls this nation has been even a greater issue that we sweep under the rug.

When Barrack Obama became the first black President in November 2008, things shifted in America. All of a sudden, for the first time in my life I saw, not all, but many whites become very afraid. It alarmed me that so many would be afraid of one election of one black president when white men in this nation had 43 elected presidents and had ran this country and its direction for 219 years. I was thinking ok; 1 out of 44, that is .02 percent of the Presidents in this country have been someone other than a white male, the world is changing and evolving, so what is the big deal? It would be a very big deal for many. It was the perception of power in the hands of a man who was not white and the jealousy over that seat of power that I would come to understand over the next eight years of his presidency. Many white's, particularly white men were afraid that they had just lost this country in which they have always claimed as their own, but no one never bother's to ask the Native Americans their opinion on that attitude, but that's another can of worms that needs to be addressed some other time. Did I always agree with all of President Barrack Obama's policies? Absolutely not, but I did acknowledge, respect and appreciate him as President of the United States as I was taught in grade school, church and in the military that we do for all Presidents in this country. In his eight years, I had never witnessed so much disregard, distain and disrespect for the President of the United States. It opened my eyes to the hearts of many people that I thought were different and were not from the error that I grew up in before I was five years old. I got to see the attitudes and realize not much had changed in 50 years.

I was used to respecting the President, it came with the office. As a child in elementary school, we had pictures of every man that had served as President of the United States posted around the walls of every classroom. It was a way of life. In fact, when I watched CNN news show over and over again on December 14th, 2008; an Iraqi journalist throw both of his shoes at the then United States President George W. Bush., I was *"smoking hot and ready to choke somebody."* Oddly enough, I realized that I had not voted for President George W. Bush, but he still was my President and no one throws their shoes at him without paying a price. I was so upset at how I had seen such disrespect for the President of the United States. It was too much for my mind to fathom. What I would find in this country when it came to a black man becoming president, not for all, but the rules would change. Now you could disrespect the president openly as a part of your "freedom of speech" your 1st Amendment right. In fact, it is no secret to the American public that on the night of President Barrack Obama's Inauguration celebration, as he danced to a song sung by national recording artist "Beyonce," that a few blocks away from the White House, 15 top Republican officials (all who are white) where having a private dinner devising a strategic plan that would under-cut the new young African American Presidency over the next four years and put power back in the hands of white men. If you don't believe me, read Robert Draper's much discussed and heavily reported book, *"Do Not Ask What Good We Do: Inside the U.S. House of Representatives."* By the way, Robert Draper is a white male and he too was born in the same error along with me, we are only 4 years apart in age. He too has seen the ugliness of greed, jealousy, politics and racism in America.

Trust me, I am not writing this to get any of us upset about racial issues, but I am going somewhere with this. I want us to

THE SPIRIT OF GREED

understand the greed for power and the jealously in man that accompanies it. Stay with me; don't jump ship now if you are still here. Fact; in September of 2009 I was scheduled to donate a kidney to my mother who had been ill for a few years. I moved temporarily to Raleigh, NC in preparation for that surgery and to assist my sister and older brother who had been looking out for her for some time. Unfortunately, mom went back into the hospital and was diagnosed too weak to have the surgery at that time. While I was visiting my mother one day at Wake Medical Hospital, the young new President Barrack Obama was in Raleigh, NC and was giving a speech locally. The speech was highly televised and the waiting room that morning in the hospital was packed with people hanging out who were visiting their family members. I too was in the waiting room at the time and when the President began to speak, almost everyone got up from their chairs to watch and listen because there where so many people standing in front of the television, although it was mounted up, you could not see over the people's head if you were sitting down. The speech last about 20 minutes or so and I noticed mother's, father's, *grandma's*, grandpa's, staff members, blacks, whites, nurses and even doctor's listening in on the speech. After the speech my attention went to a little boy who looked about 6yrs old that pulled on his mother's blouse afterwards and said *"Mommy, who is that man that everyone watching on TV?"* It was at that moment when I over-heard her response to her little boy that I saw and realized that we were not the nation that I thought we had become and surpassed what I experienced in the 1960's before I could enter kindergarten. The mother's response to her child was *"Oh, he is just somebody famous."* Now you might say, Ok Ken; what is wrong with that? I will tell you what is exactly what was wrong with that statement. First of all, I was taught in school at that age who was the President of the United

States. Not only was it wrong for her not to teach her son or withhold from her son who this man was on television; I saw at that moment that she had no intentions to ever teach her son that America has a black President. It made me wonder how many other people were doing the same thing and not to teaching their young children that Barrack Obama was President of the United States. I wonder what the President would have thought of her if he heard this mother say what she said to her little boy. This was not "Jay–Z, Tupac or 50 Cents" who are famous. This was the President of the United States! I watched this woman with my own eyes and ears, who were Caucasian, refrain from teaching her little boy who was the President of this nation. I was dumb-founded! What reasonable minded parent misses opportunities to teach their children those kinds of facts? I raised three children. I never shunned teaching opportunities like that for my sons or daughter when they asked questions like that at that age. I said to myself, "Lord, what was that all about?" At that time, I knew things were different with this black man being in office. After that, I began to notice people who couldn't and wouldn't even mention his name the entire time he was in office for eight years. What was that all about? This is painful to write, but the truth about greed for power, jealously and racism in this nation is real. I am perfectly fine with addressing it. I have lived long enough to speak on it with un-asked for skill and experience. I received my AARP on-time three years ago. I am not in the business of trying to create division, in fact; I know who I work for. I am only interested in exposing the hatred and jealousy that makes people want to try to destroy each other. This greed for power in America is not "kingdom" but "carnal." How carnal can it get in this country for power? Let's take a look at what happened in this nation throughout 2016, the raw, brutal, bitter, emotional, angry and divisive Presidential campaign between Hillary Clinton and Donald Trump. There has never in modern history in this country been a campaign so ugly. Such language, disrespect and attacks that many parents did not want their children watching the debates on television. It was certainly a lot said on both sides in attempt to destroy each other's credibility to become President. Apparently, both sides seriously thought that the nation's future was at stake and therefore the gloves where off in terms of *"throwing each other under the bus."* There was much insults said about each other from *"lock her up"*, *"to talks about Donald groping women's private parts,"* *"she being called crooked Hillary"* to *"him having small hands and reference his private part must be small as well."* I had never seen anything like it, in fact most American and the world around us had never seen anything like it. Power, greed, jealousy and the flesh for the highest office in our country was on display for the entire world to see. It was sickening. It appeared to be more of a badly written reality show than a Presidential Race. Every-day the journalist ran to report on the dual between the Republicans and the Democrats. Twitter has never gotten so much attention. By the time of the November 8, 2016 election, most Americans had been psychologically, emotionally and physically exhausted. Donald Trump would successfully tap into the fears of men and women all over America during his campaign. The fear of the country's power permanently shifting to another minority (a woman) at the helm of this country could not be fathomed. It was a big slap in the face from the American public that sent a message that still in this country *"a woman is not qualified to lead,"* Let me remind us that Deborah successfully lead Israel for 40 years as a Judge when they had no King (Judges 3:7-5:31), but that's another story. The reality is that Donald Trump understood that if he would speak to people fears (jobs, trade, undocumented immigrants, Syrian

Refugees, fighting ISIS, repealing and replacing Obama-Care and building a Mexican border wall) that men and women who were tired of government as usual would flock to him and he was right. On election night, although Hillary won the popular vote by three million people, Donald Trump decisively won the electoral vote 289 to 228. Historical blue states became blood red over-night. Just when you thought the fighting between parties would be over and Americans could get back to their personal lives, it escalated! The next day, Americans would grieve a missed opportunity to vote in its first women President right after its first African American President. The atmosphere all around the nation felt like we were standing in a funeral parlor. People were in shock everywhere. Whites, Blacks, Hispanics, Muslims, Gays, Straights, you name it. Undocumented illegal aliens were afraid of being deported. Same sex marriage couples were afraid that their marriages would be declared unconstitutional. African Americans were afraid that *"black lives wouldn't matter."* People who have lost their love one's in mass shootings, were afraid that nothing would be done to change the gun laws. Muslims in America were afraid of those who felt embolden to launch hate crimes against them and their children, to name a few issues. It was a hot mess! Just when you thought it could not get any worse we would witness protest in the streets in major cities across America and other countries against the win of President-Elect Donald Trump. There would be speculations of the legitimacy of his win since Hillary Clinton won the popular vote by over three million voters and a recount would be pursued in several states that Donald Trump won. Hold on, I'm just getting warmed up. The new President-Elect and the former President Bill Clinton, who is the husband of Hillary Clinton, took to the media punching and counter-punching each other with criticisms. The wealthy people on Wall Street the President

Elect would condemn the Clinton's for embracing during their entire political careers now became part of *"The Dream Team"* in cabinet member selection process. Talking about the *"pot calling the kettle black,"* this was interesting, 99 percent of his key leaders were billionaires, multi-millionaires and some had come directly from Wall Street itself. It gets worse. There would be reports that the new President would refuse to take part in the daily update of intelligence meetings to prepare him for what was confidential and going on around the world. He would begin to discredit the very intelligence community (CIA, FBI and NSA) and their competence in doing their jobs. He would go as far as making a statement that he would get his own personal security for he did not trust the Secret Service who have worked and served and protected all Presidents of the United States for over 200 years. Then a few days before the eve of the close of 2016 the President Barrack orders 35 Russian delegates and their families to be expelled from the United States within 72 hours for its intelligence communities facts and findings that Russian government officials at the highest level, up to Vladimir Putting had tampered, meddled and hacked into computer systems that impeded with the American voter process and subverting our democracy. Ninety-Nine House delegates on the Republican and Democratic sides saw this as unacceptable, some stating it was an *"act of war"* and Russia needed to be openly and covertly punished. Media channels all over the world would report on this new development to see where it leads. Unfortunately, the new President-Elect would still stand his ground against the competency of the American intelligence community and imply that he himself would make it the following week to be briefed by the intelligence community and their findings and express to the American public that *"its time for us to move on to better things,"* formally watering down the alleged cyberattacks by the Russian government. Now I sit here in my hotel room getting ready to go to church for Watch Service night on New Year's Eve on a short vacation to Los Angeles, California and closing out this book wondering what can we expect in the New Year (2017) when the new President takes office? I may not be able to figure that one out, but what I do know since starting this book in early 2007, greed, jealously, hatred, division and selfishness has come to a boiling point in America, even in politics. The elements of greed can and will affect those even in the highest offices of this world. That being said, it will be prudent of me to confidently declare at this time that the writings on the subject of *"The Spirit of Greed"* to be continued…..Stay Tuned!

Prayer of Salvation

Dear Readers,

This is my fourth released and published book that I have written. Many of you have read my books *Choose, Choose II, Everybody Needs a Coach and now the Spirit of Greed*. I want you to know that I appreciate your support, but I wanted to end this book and future books with a prayer of salvation to give people who have not made the Lord their savior or feel like they need to rededicate themselves to the Lord. I believe in rededication our lives back to the Lord for I found myself at the age of 26 needing to do so myself. Therefore, can you please pray this prayer below if you wanted or felt the need to dedicate your life to Christ. Who knows, you may be His next Christian author, song writer, play writer…etc.

Dear Lord,

I know that I have not been living my life according to your will and Word. I ask you to forgive me of my sins. Your word says *"If we confess with our mouth that 'Jesus Christ is Lord,' and believe that God raised him from the dead, you will be saved. For it is with your heart that you believe and are justified, and it is with your mouth that you profess your faith and are saved" (Romans 10:9-10).* Lord, I confess with my mouth that *"Jesus is Lord"* and believe in my heart that you raised him from the dead. Thank you Lord for your free gift of salvation that does not comes from works or good deeds, but comes by faith in the prayer I just said openly. In Jesus Name I seal this prayer.

    AMEN!

In Dedication and Memory of my Mother

www.ingramcontent.com/pod-product-compliance
Lightning Source LLC
Chambersburg PA
CBHW071458070526
44578CB00001B/381